MW00572580

Another Day in Paradise

Karen Telling

Michael Terence
Publishing

First published in paperback by
Michael Terence Publishing in 2021
www.mtp.agency

ISBN 9781800942134

To Nick

I couldn't, and wouldn't,
have done it without you

1

October 2003

I sat in the car and watched as Nick shut and locked the front door. It was 11 o'clock on a normal Thursday morning in early October 2003 and the neighbours had all left for work as usual. The first chill of autumn had crept into the air, leaves fell in the nearby wood and we had even noticed a touch of early morning frost.

As Nick got in the car, he sighed and looked around at the dogs snuggled into old duvets and blankets in the back. We had folded the back seat down to give them as much space as possible. They looked slightly puzzled, car journeys were normally reserved for unpleasant things like going to the vet, they weren't used to this level of space and comfort.

Nick started the car, reversed out of the drive and we turned away from our home for the last ten years. We had been very happy here in the small village he'd grown up in. We had really good neighbours in our small semi-circle of houses and regularly got together for drinks and a chat, usually on a Friday night in summer. As everyone came home from work, they'd quickly re-emerge with a bottle of beer or glass of wine in hand, ferrying bowls of crisps and peanuts and we'd all congregate on the 'green', the patch of grass in the middle of the six or seven houses and stay there until long after dusk fell. We also enjoyed the annual barbecue held in June or July; invariably it would rain but we'd shelter under a selection of gazebos and watch the chefs cook under umbrellas, whilst the rest of us produced salad, fresh baguettes, baked potatoes and home-made - or perhaps, artfully distressed - supermarket desserts. It wasn't easy to leave but we'd made up our minds.

We headed up the High Street and found a parking space close to our immediate destination. As we walked in, a young man came towards us, smiling,

"Everything Ok Mr Telling?" he said, shaking Nick's hand. "When's the big day?"

We had already exchanged contracts on our house but completion would take a few weeks, so we had decided not to wait and just get going.

We looked at each other, then gestured to the car, visible through the office window. He followed our gaze and took in the roof box, the two dogs, not daring to take their eyes off us and then at the keys in Nick's hand.

"We're off now," said Nick.

A look of disbelief crossed the young man's face and his smile faltered.

"Now?"

"Yes," I replied. "We're leaving for Portugal today!"

We walked out of the estate agent's office, got back into the car and Nick started the engine. With just enough packed into the roof box to get us through the next three or four days travelling, we headed out of the village and onto the motorway, next stop Folkestone. This promised to be a very different experience from our first trip to Portugal and I couldn't help my mind returning to those heady, carefree days of sixteen years ago. The past suddenly seemed incredibly important. Had I known what our future would bring, that I would find myself lying in a hospital bed, not knowing if I would ever walk or even sit upright again, I wonder now if we would have embarked on this venture at all. But hindsight, as they say, is a wonderful thing.

2

1987 – Portugal First Time Around

A friend had just invested in a holiday home in Portugal and offered it to us any time we wanted a break. We had never been to Portugal, never even considered it. We enjoyed holidays in France, Croatia, Italy and even a few trips to Florida but the resort sounded appealing, so we decided to take him up on his kind offer. We arrived at Gatwick before dawn, coincidentally on my birthday. As we headed through customs and passport control, a young woman with a bright smile and a clipboard popped up.

"Can you spare a minute to answer a few questions?"

At 5.30 in the morning, I couldn't guarantee it.

"Can we start with your date of birth?" she chirped.

I stared at her blankly. Nick shook his head with a mixture of amusement and then disbelief as it dawned on him.

"It's today!" he exclaimed.

The girl's face fell as she looked from him to me, unsure who should win the prize as Idiot No.1.

"Oh yes," I said, lamely. "So it is."

She looked enthusiastic but how on earth could I answer her questions if I didn't even know it was my birthday?

We managed to dodge the survey and after a quick trip to Boots to stock up on insect repellent and sunscreen and a breakfast of coffee and a croissant, I headed to WH Smith for a browse through the paperbacks. A holiday isn't a holiday for me without a solid stack of fresh, new books, half a dozen at least to last the week. The hardest part is always deciding where to start first, like opening a box of delicious chocolates.

A glance at the overhead screen showed the gate number for the flight to Faro and we joined our fellow passengers on the interminable walk along the airport corridor. The flight took off on time and proved uneventful, apart from the slightly hair-raising descent, where we believed we would land on the sea but at the last minute the runway came into view and with a gentle bump, we hit land. The sky looked so blue, not a cloud anywhere. As we stepped out of the plane, the heat swarmed over us and a slight shimmering haze hovered above the tarmac, all before 10 o'clock in the morning. We'd left a chilly autumnal morning and just over two hours later, emerged into a summer's day.

The whole place felt deserted apart from the buzz around our arrival and each side of the runway looked more like a beach and a lake than an airport. The ground crew, stylish even in their hi-vis jackets, welcomed us to the Algarve. We had no idea of the significance of that first visit, it was just a last chance to catch some sun and chill out before the onset of the freezing temperatures and foggy gloom of an English winter.

At the foot of the steps from the plane, we queued to get onto one of the waiting buses, engines pumping out diesel fumes, while passengers rounded up bags and children, most of us already overheating in our thick jumpers and heavy coats. The bus looked full to me, all the seats occupied, but more and more passengers squashed on until there was no standing room either. It didn't matter whether you had a strap to hang onto, we were so tightly packed in, there was no chance of falling. The bus lurched away from the plane but we couldn't see anything resembling a terminal building, just some sheds with corrugated metal roofs. As we drew closer, we could make out FARO proudly spelt out in big white letters.

The bus stopped suddenly and we realised the shed was actually the terminal building. We gathered our hand luggage and waited to leave the bus and join the queue for passport control. Behind the desk sat a solitary, bored-looking official, slowly checking passports. We shuffled along while he studied each one intently, then stared at its owner, then back at the passport. He seemed constantly surprised, and more than a little disappointed, that each one was valid. Maybe he longed for a little excitement in his job. At last, it was our turn to be scrutinised; he reluctantly handed our passports over with a heavy sigh and gestured for us to join the growing line to his right. We grabbed a trolley and wandered over, expecting to see a conveyor belt, groaning with luggage but only discovered a row of shelves, two high, and behind them strips of plastic curtains, of the type used in a doorway, to keep flies out. Suddenly we heard a vehicle draw up and the engine idled, humming away, as pairs of hands pushed through the plastic strips and placed our suitcases onto the waiting shelves. We all had to walk up and down, anxiously trying to spot our cases. We had never been to an airport where the passengers moved and the luggage sat motionless. Everyone tripped over everyone else, retrieving bags, pushchairs and random pieces of luggage, whilst trolleys clashed and tangled themselves in other people's belongings. It was chaotic and we felt grateful no other flight had come in at the same time. I couldn't imagine the drama in high summer; no wonder that system didn't catch on.

We successfully navigated the baggage hall and exited the shed, following the signs for our car hire company and soon set off on the open road. Our destination, a former fishing village called Praia do Carvoeiro, lay 50 Km to the west along the N125, the Algarve's 'Road of Death' with the highest number of fatalities in Europe. You could tell the tourists, driving carefully, obeying all the road signs, from the locals, swaying from verge to verge, arms out of windows, all hands off the steering wheel to light cigarettes. As we witnessed overtaking at the last minute, overtaking a car already overtaking, on a bend, on a hill, it grew increasingly obvious how the N125 had earned its grisly reputation.

Finally, we made it to the village, by now it was mid-morning and the temperature rising well into the 20s. We looked ridiculous dressed up for a UK autumn, and couldn't wait to change into something more appropriate for the climate. Our directions told us to turn off the main road, down towards the sea and through the small village streets which led to the stunning beach, a beautiful curved bay with cliffs on either side. We crossed the small village square, not at all sure who had right of way as four or five roads led into the square and it looked like a free for all. We glimpsed the rolling waves through the confusion of parked cars and market stalls at the edge of the square, the latter selling brightly coloured clothes, beach towels and traditional lace tablecloths. Beyond the stalls stood a couple of bars and restaurants, already busy with tourists drinking in the sun, the view of the ocean, the atmosphere – and the local beer and wine.

Checking the directions, we turned up the steep hill to one side of the beach, along a road flanked by shops, bars and restaurants. Families strolled down towards the beach, laden with buckets and spades and cool boxes full of picnics. Most stopped and studied the menus outside the restaurants, deciding where to eat that evening. We carried on up the hill; however, at the top, where our directions said turn right, we couldn't find a signpost for the development. We turned off anyway, hoping to come across it and found ourselves on the headland which curved along the cliff top then dropped down and of course, we found ourselves back at the beach.

We checked the directions once more, up the hill, turn right and into the development, so we set off again thinking we must have missed the turning. Back up the hill, past the same families looking in the same restaurants, we scoured every signpost and every turning only to arrive back at the headland again. We must have gone wrong, but couldn't work out where. Back down to the beach, back up the hill, almost on nodding terms with the beach-bound families, feeling quite at home here now but this time we decided to keep going further on.

The early start combined with the heat and the confusion over the directions hardly created the happiest of atmospheres in the car. This time we didn't turn off at the cliff top but kept on up a steep, winding road edged with white-painted villas, which became more and more sparse. How could we have gone wrong again? It's a small village and we were looking for a fairly large complex of apartments, villas, tennis courts, restaurants, swimming pools - where could it have gone? Was it an Algarvean Brigadoon, only appearing every 25 years in the mist?

Nowhere to turn off existed, so we motored on. Suddenly we rounded a corner and faced a sheer drop with no barrier and our road skimming the cliff edge. We gasped and looked at each other, what a nightmare! We were in the middle of nowhere, no sign of our villa and threatened with instant death at any minute over a cliff. We should have stayed at home. The road straightened out and we climbed even further uphill until I felt sure we had to be back in Faro, then suddenly, up reared a huge billboard, bearing the words we had longed for: Rocha Brava. We had arrived.

The villa looked lovely; it stood in a quiet spot, down a shady footpath just a few minutes' walk to the pool, according to the map handed to us when we checked in. We unlocked the door and put our cases down with a huge sigh of relief, at last, our holiday could begin. We quickly changed into shorts and t-shirts, dug the flip flops out of the case and went for a stroll around the complex. It was beautiful, with hibiscus and oleander flowers everywhere in all shades from delicate pink to robust red and striking purple. The pool was huge, set on different levels with a waterfall in between and surrounded by loungers draped with sunbathers. The original farm building overlooked it, now converted into an attractive restaurant with a large terrace. The stresses of the journey started to fade away and we relaxed into the holiday mood.

Later in the evening, we got ready to head back into the village to investigate those restaurants we had passed earlier, making sure to leave plenty of time for the long drive. We turned left out of the development and almost immediately found ourselves back at the dangerous bend, at least this time we were on the inside and Nick hugged the rock face of the cliff that jutted upwards to our right. Around a couple of bends and suddenly we arrived back at the top of the hill where we had taken the wrong turn twice that morning. How could we have reached it so quickly? We only left the villa five minutes ago. It's so strange how once you are familiar with a road it seems to take no time at all.

We carried on down the hill; cars filled the parking spaces on both sides of the road. It was late in the season but still very busy and parking obviously came at a premium. Suddenly, Nick swung the car off to the right and squeezed into a narrow gap, the only one available for miles and parked right outside a restaurant called Casa Algarvia. The waiters stood outside, with their arms folded and unsmiling; they looked vaguely intimidating. It was still quite early as we had expected a much longer drive and although we could see lots of people walking up and down and studying menus, the restaurants were only just starting to fill up. We weren't sure if these spaces belonged to the restaurant, given every other space was already taken and whether we could just walk off, so we looked at the menu displayed in a glass case on the wall. The waiters watched us approach, no friendlier than before, but the food looked interesting so we stepped up onto the terrace and immediately they broke out into wide smiles, reaching to shake Nick's hand and guide us to a corner table.

The week fled by, the holiday a dream, one of the best we'd ever had. We tried as many of the restaurants as we could and none disappointed. We walked on the beach, swam in the pool and relaxed on the terrace. The sun shone every day, the locals were extremely friendly and it just felt perfect. As we drove through the square on our last morning, on the way back to Faro airport, I gazed up at the blue sky, said goodbye to the beach and knew this would not be my last time here.

3

October 2003 (continued)

Sixteen years later, we arrived at the Eurotunnel terminal and showed our passports. The paperwork we had meticulously prepared for the dogs, in accordance with DEFRA regulations, was completely ignored and we drove straight onto the train. Portugal awaited and the start of our new life.

The journey to Calais proved uneventful and as we disembarked in France, I waited for someone to stop us and check our documents.

"When do they check the paperwork?" I asked after we'd driven for about five minutes.

Nick looked at me, puzzled.

"We're way past any customs or border officials."

"So that's it?"

"Yes," he replied.

What an anti-climax.

We'd booked a room in an Ibis hotel in Arras, just south of Calais, all Ibis hotels are pet friendly. It wasn't easy to find and we seemed trapped in a maze of narrow, one-way streets. We kept glimpsing flashes of the illuminated hotel sign but couldn't work out how to get to it. When we finally achieved it, we had to unload the dogs and all their accessories, plus our overnight bags onto the pavement. I attempted to check in while Nick disappeared into the night in search of somewhere to leave the car. This was even more of an adventure for Gem and Samson, they had never been in a hotel before, never mind a lift that took us up to our second-floor room.

Gem, a rescued German Shepherd cross, was 14 and quite laid-back, probably because she was losing her hearing and her sight. We'd adopted her when she was about 18 months old; her black muzzle had now turned completely grey. We hadn't even expected her to make the journey to Portugal as she had several health problems and was none too steady on her back legs, but it seemed she was determined to accompany us to our new home. As she plodded on and as our moving date drew closer, we had to quickly get her paperwork and vaccinations sorted so she could join us on our adventure.

Samson, a beautiful golden retriever, was known as 'helium dog'. He had never really grown out of puppyhood and was flighty and skittish. He would suddenly leap into the air during a walk, at some scary event, real or imagined, and we had no idea how he would react to all these new experiences. Nick returned, having had to leave the car where he could, fingers crossed it would still be there in the morning. We gathered up our scattered belongings and managed to get us all safely into our room.

It was dark now, about 7 pm. Not wanting to leave an elderly matron with uncertain bladder control and a 7-year-old, masquerading as an unpredictable pup, alone, we trooped back down in the lift and went out to find somewhere to eat. Not far from the hotel we came across two magnificent squares surrounded by impressive, grand baroque buildings. We could see several restaurants and decided on the closest one, choosing to sit at an outside table, despite the slight chill in the air, and to the obvious amusement of the waitress. We ordered ham and cheese omelettes and a bottle of wine, to toast the start of our journey south. The dogs settled under the table and although we had fed them at the hotel, they were more than happy to share our omelettes and were better behaved than I had ever seen them before. We all slept well that night, Gem snoring on her bed on the floor and Samson sandwiched between us, making sure we couldn't leave without him.

At 6 am, Gem woke up, ready for her morning constitutional, so we all stumbled out into the darkness, searching for a piece of grass that she would deem suitable to pee on. Green space seemed to be in very short supply, but eventually, we saw a patch across the road, only realising once we got there that it was actually a mini-roundabout and early morning commuters found themselves treated to the sight of Gem relieving her bladder as they made their way to work.

The car had come to no harm, so we loaded dogs and bags and started back on our way. Unfortunately, we took a wrong turn somewhere along the motorway and ended up on the Paris Périphérique, something like the M25, only busier and with more junctions. Somehow, we always managed to get trapped in the wrong lane at each exit, so we went around and around, both of us becoming increasingly stressed, voices growing increasingly clipped and higher-pitched, strained silences punctuated with cries of:

"Is it this one?"

"Quick, over there!"

"Damn, missed it," and around we'd go again.

Suddenly I spotted a gap in the traffic. I checked the map (no sat nav then!)

"Quick, take that exit," I shouted.

Nick indicated and swung across onto the slip road and then the dual carriageway; the relief, we had escaped. We craned our necks to read the next signpost, we had a choice of returning to the Périphérique or heading for… the centre of Paris.

Having longed to get off the Périphérique we now couldn't wait to get back on it before we found ourselves at the Arc de Triomphe. However, we had to carry on until we came to a roundabout so we could retrace our steps and throw ourselves back into the meleé. This time we were calmer, eyes on the prize, slowly moving across the lanes as we circled Paris and finally, success. The right exit, going in the right direction and it had only cost us an hour and a half. Back on the right road, we breathed a sigh of relief and relaxed as the French countryside sped past, surely the worst was over, we were really on our way now.

A couple of hours later as we coasted through a lovely part of France, heading for a hotel just outside Toulouse, I noticed Nick looked tense, pumping the accelerator pedal and frowning.

"What's wrong?" I asked. No reply. "What is it?"

"Hmmm. Just don't seem to have any power."

We were climbing uphill on the motorway and I could feel the car pulling back. Nick had his foot on the floor but what should have been an easy incline was proving to be a struggle. It was Friday afternoon and we had no idea where to find the nearest VW garage. We took a chance and left at the next exit in the hope of getting some help. We followed the signs to the nearest town all the time wondering would we find a garage?

Would they have the parts we needed? Would we be stuck in the middle of France for the weekend with two dogs?

We trundled into the town square; everywhere seemed deserted. We turned down a road at random, but there wasn't a soul to be seen. We appeared to be heading out of town, so we turned around and tried another route. This looked more promising, with a few signs of life, what looked like an industrial estate and yes, a petrol station.

The guy behind the counter looked perplexed as I tried to explain. Unfortunately, the workings of the internal combustion engine hadn't featured prominently in my O level exams. He scratched his head, glanced at the car, then picked up the phone, dialled and spoke quickly into the receiver. The conversation was brief and as he finished speaking, he looked at us, raised his index finger and gestured towards the car with a nod of his head. We went back to the car and waited, and waited, the clock moving closer to 4 pm. The air felt warm, heavy, still and almost silent, no passing traffic, not even a dog barking. We still had several hours to go before reaching our destination. I started to wonder whether we should cancel our booking but I didn't hold out much hope of finding alternative accommodation here.

We took the dogs for a walk but saw hardly anyone else as we did a circuit of the square. We looked in the shop windows as we passed, most of them covered in thick yellow plastic to protect the displays from the damaging power of the sun. There was a chemist, with intriguing rows of plain-ish boxes of unknown lotions and potions; a clothes shop with the latest fashion from about 1978, not exactly Parisian haute couture; an empty bar, the waiter industriously drying glasses with a pristine tea towel, obviously anticipating a rush of customers.

Having exhausted the fairly meagre entertainment opportunities, we wandered back to the car and were amazed to see it surrounded by an animated group of men, all of whom seemed to have an opinion on the cause of our predicament. One stepped forward, shook Nick's hand and gestured for him to open the bonnet. He spoke a little English and with the help of mime, we managed to demonstrate the car going uphill slower and slower, while Nick pressed harder and harder on the accelerator. The little group eagerly gathered around the engine and set about checking everything and anything that could be easily pulled out or pushed in or twisted or turned. I just hoped they knew what they were doing. After about half an hour of investigations, the bonnet was slammed shut and several greasy hands slapped and patted it. The self-appointed spokesman stepped forward, two black thumbs raised.

"Ok," he smiled.

"Really?" said Nick in total disbelief.

"Oui, Ok."

More sign language and stilted French and English followed but we got the gist that there was nothing drastically wrong that would stop us from continuing our journey. Although wary of getting back on the road, we didn't have much choice. As far as the guys in front of us were concerned, whatever had caused the lack of power wasn't serious. Nick went to take his wallet out of his back pocket but was waved away by grubby, oily hands.

"No, nothing!"

We couldn't just drive off, six of them had spent ages checking the car over, but if they wouldn't accept money, what should we do? Nick strode off to the bar we had passed earlier, explained the situation to the best of his ability and on the barman's recommendation, returned with bottles of beer and a bottle of Pastis. The clinking carrier bags provoked a lively response, much smiling, laughing, and slapping of Nick on the back. One of the men produced a small bottle-opener key ring and set about opening the beers and passing them around. The owner of the petrol station disappeared and returned with a jug of water and an assortment of mismatched cups, mugs and glasses. Another few slaps on the back and shouts of 'santé' and we slid back into the car nervously. We decided to take them at their word and head for the hotel, leaving the start of a very high-spirited looking party behind us. I wonder what their wives/girlfriends/mothers thought when they rolled home that evening: 'So there was this English couple...and they bought you beers and Pastis...right...? I can't imagine it was a regular occurrence in their small, sleepy town.

Thankfully the car behaved itself, still not over-powerful, but it kept going until we gratefully turned into the car park of the hotel. Another dog-friendly place, this time in a large open field, with the rumble of the motorway off in the distance. The staff were very accommodating. We could sit in the lounge/bar area with the dogs and they even brought a large bowl of water and placed it under the table where Gem and Samson had made themselves comfortable. We'd only been on the road for just over 24 hours, but they had already adapted to the massive change in their normal routine. As long as they were with us, they felt fine and looked every bit the seasoned travellers, snoozing by our feet in their second French hotel.

The next morning, we loaded the car once again. We planned on making a detour to a small village I had visited often, more than 20 years ago, to stay with my French pen pal, Anne. After a couple of hours on the road, the car still chugging along, we arrived at Foix, recognisable even after all these years. We turned off the main road and plunged deep into the Pyrenean countryside. Nothing to see for miles except fields, trees and the huge, craggy mountains looming up in the distance.

A few houses appeared on either side of the road, which widened as we approached the village. The petrol station was still there on the right-hand side, then a small cafe, a few more houses and we arrived in the square. Straight ahead, I could see the only other cafe in town, where we had spent so much time as teenagers. We whiled away most of our summer afternoons playing table football, with 'Bette Davis Eyes' on repeat on the jukebox and ordering Menthe a l'eau and citron pressé. Nothing seemed to have changed at all. We took the dogs for a quick walk around. We saw the post office, the butcher, the general store, all so familiar as if I had just left yesterday. We had lunch at the cafe, sitting outside on the terrace with the dogs at our feet as was becoming usual. So many happy memories came flooding back, it didn't seem possible that more than two decades had passed.

After lunch, we drove around to the other side of the village, where the farmland began again and there stood Anne's parents' house. I had no idea if they still lived there, and if so, would they even recognise or remember me? I walked up to the front door and knocked, but there was no reply and no sign of life inside. I felt disappointed but also a tiny bit relieved. It would have been very awkward if they had no idea who we were, plus we really needed to get back on the road; our next hotel reservation was in Valencia and we still had the Pyrenees to cross.

4

The 1990s – A Holiday

For the first time ever, we had gone back to the same place on holiday, back to the same complex in Carvoeiro. I couldn't explain the attraction to the place but it just felt so easy and natural, like coming home. We started to visit more frequently, taking long weekends away from running our business, any opportunity to go back to this little village. We had started renting detached villas with private pools, not an easy thing to do back in the late 80s/early 90s. Instead of a few clicks on a screen, we searched the classified ads in The Lady magazine. There were quite a few villas in Carvoeiro, so we would phone the number given, then wait for a small hand-made brochure to arrive in the post. It usually consisted of several sheets of paper, with actual photos glued on showing the accommodation and pool area. This was all we had to go on when deciding where to book, no reviews or google maps to help us make up our minds. Fortunately, they were all lovely places and we found a few that became firm favourites, that we returned to time and time again. Even being burgled on one visit didn't stop us.

It happened on the penultimate night of our stay in a detached villa on the outskirts of the village when we arrived home to find broken glass and passports and cash missing. We called the local Guarda Nacional Republicana, or GNR, the National Guard of Portugal, who came and had a look around but didn't offer much hope of catching the criminals. In fact, they showed more interest in inspecting the huge bar of

Toblerone we had bought at Duty-Free on the way over.

For the last night of our stay, we had booked a table back at Casa Algarvia, but we felt so shattered after a busy day making police reports and hurriedly replacing passports at the local consulate in Portimao, we couldn't really face leaving the villa again. We called in to explain to the head waiter, João, and to cancel our reservation. As we told him the story, his face fell, he was horrified and embarrassed at what had happened and just kept shaking his head sadly.

"But you are friends of Algarve."

We reassured him we would remain friends of Algarve but we would just stay in the villa that evening, and anyway, we had an early flight and still had to pack. I saw his face light up.

"You come tonight," he said, patting Nick on the shoulder. "You eat what you want, you drink what you want, you pay me next time."

He obviously assumed that we had lost all our money and credit cards. It was such a lovely gesture and to think that we found him intimidating when we parked outside on the first night of our first holiday.

Many years ago, there was only one road into the village, just wide enough for a horse and cart and no more. However, once the traditional mode of transport gave way to cars and lorries, it became a one-way street, the 'in' road, and a parallel path became the 'out' road. Between the two stood a row of buildings, most of which had originally been fishermen's cottages, but now housed shops, restaurants, and cafes. One of our favourites was Casa Chá. Inside, it looked tiny, with space for about four tables, but outside on the pavement, there were about a dozen. It was so popular that a queue would form from about 10 o'clock each morning. They served the most delicious coffee and freshly squeezed orange juice, and a limited breakfast menu. The cooked options consisted of scrambled or boiled eggs on toast. However, the kitchen was so small and they only had one gas ring, so if you didn't want to still be there at lunchtime, you had to decide that everyone at the table had either boiled or scrambled.

Closer to our villa, down a rough track, we discovered Chicken George. The restaurant formed part of his house and the bar area was more like his living room. His father sat in front of the television, oblivious to the customers wandering in and out. It boasted Formica tables and hard chairs inside, and outside a covered terrace with long lines of benches pulled up to wooden tables. George tended the barbecue out in the car park with a hairdryer rigged up and aimed at the charcoal to keep the flames going, whilst the chicken browned and crisped on the grill and George basted the skin with the fiery Piri-Piri marinade. On our first visit, we turned up and placed our order for chicken, chips and salad. George looked at us expectantly.

"Where pots?"

"Sorry?"

"Where pots?" he repeated. "You bring pots."

Leaving us none the wiser.

"We don't have pots," I ventured, arms raised, showing pot-less hands.

George smiled at our naivety and shook his head.

"Chicken, take away, you bring many pots," and he mimed

filling containers with chicken and walking away.

The penny dropped.

"Oh, we bring you pots, for chicken?"

"Yes," he grinned, holding up two Piri-Piri coloured fingers. "Two people, small pot," his hands now cupped, to form a small bowl. "Eight people, big pot," he moved his hands wide apart. "Chips, two people, small pot; salad, two people, small pot."

"Ok, we have to come back, with pots."

"Yes, yes, bring many pots."

We got into the car and headed back to our villa. We hadn't even looked in the kitchen cupboards and had no idea of how many pots we had - or whether they were two-people small pots or eight-people big pots. We found a mismatched set of dishes, in glass, china and pottery and managed to cobble together three that looked roughly similar in size. Then we headed back down the winding track. As we pulled into the car park, George was still there at the barbecue and we saw another couple of tourists standing talking to him. As we drew nearer, we could hear the familiar word: "Pots." We strode up confidently. George turned to us and beamed.

"Pots," he said, turning to the other couple. "Look, pots!"

He snatched the dishes from us and disappeared into the bar area. We followed and watched as he handed them over to his kitchen assistant. She set each one on the weighing scales on the counter, zeroed the scales, then started filling them with freshly cooked chips, a salad of sliced tomato and onion, sprinkled with olive oil and oregano and the golden pieces of chicken. Each dish was then covered in foil and placed in a plastic bag, while

George calculated the price. We realised now why we had to bring our own pots. He priced the food by the kilo, so whatever sized dishes you brought, he filled up and that's what you paid for. I don't know how our local chippy would have coped with that system, but it made perfect sense here.

5

2003 – The Road to A New Life

Another night, another dog-friendly Ibis hotel, this time close to Valencia airport. We had the routine down to a fine art now, dogs out for a quick walk to stretch their legs, check into the hotel and deposit our few bits of luggage in the room, then back out for a longer walk and something to eat for all four of us. We were all getting used to life on the road and I had actually forgotten why we were doing it, but tomorrow we should reach our destination. The reality suddenly hit me; we weren't on holiday, we didn't have a home to go back to in the UK, what on earth were we thinking?

We set off again early the next morning and by mid-afternoon, crossed the border into Portugal. It was a beautiful, hot, sunny afternoon, incredibly warm compared to the temperatures we had left behind. The road became familiar once we passed Faro and we started to see familiar landmarks like the billboard of a cup of coffee, a 'bica', which stood on the main road from the airport. This time we weren't in a hire car and for the first time, we had the dogs with us. I had spent so many holidays just wishing we didn't have to leave them behind, thinking it would be just perfect if they could come with us, and now they were. Forty-five minutes later, we took the turn-off to Carvoeiro, the last few miles, back on home territory.

By now, we had bought an apartment in Carvoeiro and although plenty big enough to live in, it was on the 3rd and 4th floors of the building, and not really suitable for the dogs. Plus, it provided our only source of income now, so we had rented a 4-bedroom, detached villa with a garden and a pool, for 6 months through the winter. We had only seen photos of the place, but it looked fine. It had 4 bathrooms, gas central heating and a log burner, a fully equipped kitchen and only a few minutes' walk from the village, perfect.

The road up to the villa seemed steeper than we had imagined, much steeper. We found the villa. It did have a lovely big garden, obviously very well-tended, but the gravel drive rose up another steep incline which curved around the house, finishing by the front door, located at the back. We found the key, cunningly hidden under the doormat and let ourselves in. What had appeared to be a rather grand wooden staircase in the photos we had seen, looked rather less impressive in real life. It was scuffed and dented and the handrail wobbled alarmingly. The marble floor tiles had long since lost their shine and some had chipped corners.

Double glass doors opened up to a large living/dining room with patio doors along the length of one wall, which in turn opened onto a huge balcony, looking down onto the garden and across the valley beyond. However, the patio doors rattled and were so badly fitting, we had to push and drag them open, instead of gliding them on their runners. A beautiful, marble and glass dining table stood at one end of the room, but the sagging, threadbare sofas had seen better days. Everywhere we looked, loomed almost life-size, dark, carved, wooden, statues, like in some kind of Hammer Horror mansion.

We explored further and found 3 bedrooms on this floor, which all smelt damp and musty, despite the brilliant sunshine outside. One of them had an en-suite bathroom, so we decided to make that ours. We found a small shower room, placed directly between the living room and the kitchen. The shower curtain hung precariously from half a dozen hooks, on a crooked, plastic rail, and although technically you could count two doors between loo and kitchen, you could almost pour out your morning cup of tea whilst still brushing your teeth.

Upstairs, another damp bedroom and bathroom greeted us and a private terrace with broken, mossy, floor tiles and a rusty table and chairs. The whole house seemed to have been lying empty for years but we knew that holidaymakers had only just left. I couldn't imagine what they made of it. Back in the living room, Nick couldn't stand it a moment longer and began turning all the statues to face the wall, even the one reclining on the chaise longue at the back of the room. That would have to do for now, but they couldn't stay in the living room permanently. It was like being surrounded by a silent audience, watching our every move.

We heard a knock at the door, followed by a shout.

"Hello!"

And in walked Terry, the house manager. We had only communicated via email before and I hadn't expected him to be quite so, well, English. From his Manchester United replica football shirt to his socks and open sandals, he looked the picture of the archetypal Brit abroad.

"Great, you've arrived; all ok? Did you have a good journey?" he boomed in his flat, nasal voice.

"Erm, yes," I hesitated, but with the usual British talent for understatement, added, "everything's fine."

"Jolly good, well, make yourselves at home. Maria, the maid will be in in the morning and Fernando, the gardener and pool man, comes Wednesdays and Saturdays."

"What days does Maria come?" I asked.

"Every day," he replied cheerily. "Every weekday at 9 for about 3 hours; she'll do the washing up, change the beds, towels, clean the floors, windows, all that sort of thing."

"Every day?" I questioned; we hadn't banked on a part-time housekeeper. "It's not really necessary, you know, we're not on holiday. So, we just want to live normally, and we don't have a cleaner, normally." I was conscious of gabbling, but couldn't seem to stop.

"But she gets paid all through the winter anyway, so she might as well come," he said, looking confused.

"But if she gets paid anyway, she might as well have the winter off?" I suggested tentatively, trying to catch Nick's eye, but his attention lay elsewhere, still wrestling with the statues, who seemed none too keen on facing the wall and had decided to put up a fight.

"Nah, mate, what will she do all winter if she doesn't have her work to keep her going?" Terry shook his head. "Maria's cleaned this house every day for, oh must be more than 20 years. It's her life, she wouldn't know what to do with a week off, never mind a whole winter!"

He chuckled to himself incredulously. He obviously thought I was mad, wanting to pass up the opportunity of so much help around the house, but I'm not good at sharing my privacy. I don't want to feel that I have to be up and showered and dressed by 9 o'clock every morning if I want to just chill out and read a book in my pyjamas. I decided to let it go for now and try to talk to Maria when she arrived the next morning. Maybe she would be pleased to have a bit of a break.

"Got to be off now. You know, places to go, people to see," Terry winked. "Beer to drink, ha ha!" He obviously found himself hilarious. "Any problems, give me a call," and he wandered off whistling.

I turned to Nick.

"Did you hear that?"

"What?"

"About Maria, the maid?"

He put down the semi-naked statue, which wobbled precariously then crashed to the ground.

"These bloody statues, not one of them's got two legs the same length!"

"Maria, the maid," I repeated. "She comes in every day, EVERY DAY!"

"Does she? What does she do?"

"Everything, every bloody thing; the place won't feel like it's ours. We'll have to be up and ready as if we were going to work. I had hoped we could have a kind of extended holiday. We'll have a bit of money in the bank once the house sale completes next week, and after all the stress of sorting it all out and moving over, I thought we could relax, chill out, for a few months at least."

"A few months," he looked horrified. "Really, a few MONTHS?"

"Yes, why, what were you thinking?"

"Oh, a couple of weeks. I've never been unemployed before."

I looked at him in disbelief.

"You're not unemployed now, you numpty."

We had sold our business a few months ago in preparation for the move and even though he'd insisted on doing night shifts, shelf-stacking at a local supermarket, I didn't think he'd be so keen on starting work. Anyway, we had no idea of what kind of work we were going to do, apart from holiday lets in the apartment.

"We'll talk about it later," he said. "Just give me a hand with the rest of these statues."

On our first evening in our new home, we took the dogs for a walk, then decided to try leaving them alone for an hour or two while we walked down to the village for a drink and something to eat. We would need to go shopping tomorrow. It felt strange not having a single piece of food in the house, no five-year-old jars of herbs at the back of the cupboard, or half-empty bottles of pickled onions in the fridge. It hadn't actually registered before, that we were starting completely from scratch.

As we walked down the hill, everything felt totally different. It was so lovely to be back and no longer as tourists but as locals. After a stroll around the square by the beach, a glass of wine for me and an 'imperial' or small beer for Nick, we suddenly felt exhausted and decided to just get some chicken Piri-Piri and chips and a bottle of delicious local wine to take back to the villa. Sitting out on the front balcony, dogs at our feet, as usual, the evening grew dark and as we finished our meal and last of the wine, Nick sighed.

"We're actually here, can you believe it, living the dream!"

6

The Dream Becomes Reality

The next morning, I woke early, it was only 6.30 and the room was in complete darkness, thanks to the heavy wooden shutters, fixed firmly at the window. I crept out to the kitchen and let the dogs out for a sniff around their new garden. A narrow gravel path at the back of the house led to a low, dry-stone retaining wall, only a couple of feet high. Above that, stretched a piece of completely wild, open land, full of long grass and almond and fig trees. The wall was so low that anyone could easily jump down and be straight into our garden. I hadn't realised when we arrived yesterday that it was so exposed.

The dogs were wandering around, keen to investigate their new surroundings when I heard a whistle, then footsteps and a man and his two dogs appeared walking towards the wall. He was probably in his 30s, dressed casually in jeans and a jumper and both dogs were off the lead, one a rottweiler, the other a husky-type. I was suddenly terrified. What if the dogs saw ours and jumped down to attack them? Ours were such softies and Gem was so old, I wouldn't have a hope of fighting them off.

I quickly called the dogs in but they studiously ignored me, much more interested in all the fascinating scents. I grabbed their collars and dragged them inside, then watched from the kitchen window as the rottweiler and husky stood on top of the wall and sniffed the air; they could obviously tell there were strangers in town. Their owner sauntered over and looked down into the garden too; they were all just 6 feet or so from the front door. He gave a command and all three turned and wandered back across the field.

Maybe this house had been a mistake. How could I relax and let the dogs wander around outside when anyone, or any dog, could just appear like that, with no fence between us? Nick was up now too, I must have made more noise than I thought, so I explained about the man and the dogs.

"Oh, I'm sure they'll be fine," he said. "He wouldn't have them off the lead if they were dangerous, just relax."

Oh yes, just relax, with the hounds of the Baskervilles ready to attack my precious babies at any moment. We had been married for 15 years; did he not know me at all?

Of course, the perfect antidote to any emergency is a nice cup of tea and Nick had found a dusty pack of teabags in one of the cupboards, probably left behind by previous holidaymakers. He made us both a cup (no milk or sugar for him for the first time ever) and as it was now fully light, we went back outside. The man and his dogs had gone and with no sign of any other potential intruders, and my drama-llama reputation intact, we started exploring. To the right, we spotted another low wall with a wrought-iron gate set into it and on the other side, a huge swimming pool, although like the rest of the house, badly in need of maintenance. The pool tiles and those that surrounded it appeared cracked and dirty. It was such a shame because this house could be spectacular with a bit of time and TLC spent on it.

A little face appeared on the other side of the boundary wall between us and the next-door neighbours, attracted by the sound of our voices and we saw a small grey and white tabby cat with huge bright blue eyes. We had always had dogs but never cats, and both the dogs absolutely hated them. When we took them for walks around our home in England, they spent most of the time darting under parked cars and peering down driveways, hoping to spy a cat so they could bark at them and pretend to give chase, even though they were always firmly on their leads. Some of the neighbourhood cats delighted in taunting them by sitting on top of the fence panels in our garden, calmly washing or sitting in the sun while the dogs went ballistic below. Once again, I quickly ushered the dogs back inside; Rottweilers, huskies and now cats, they would never be able to go out unaccompanied again.

Back inside, I glanced at the clock, 8.45, how was it that time already? Maria would be here in 15 minutes and I still had to shower and dress and tidy up. We hadn't brought much with us;

a friend was following in a couple of weeks with all our belongings in his van, but what clothes we had were strewn about the bedroom, and everything else lay dumped where we'd left it the previous evening.

I hurried into the bathroom, ignoring the delightful decor. Each bathroom sported tiles of a different colour; this one was dysentery beige. The bath felt rough beneath my feet, it either needed re-enamelling or descaling, but I didn't have time to investigate further. The hot water gurgled through the pipes and drummed loudly on the side of the bath, while I had the quickest shower and hair wash ever. I stepped out and wrapped a towel around me, then wound another smaller one around my head and went back into the bedroom, to find a short, stout woman opening the shutters and flooding the room with sunlight.

"Bom dia!" she greeted me, bustling past and starting to make the bed, while I stood and stared, water dripping in a puddle around me.

"Bom dia," I replied shakily. I guessed I'd just met Maria.

She was totally unperturbed by my semi-naked appearance, while I just stood there rooted to the spot. Eventually, she left and I could start to get dressed. I could still hear her in the living room next door, humming away tunelessly as she worked.

I joined Nick in the kitchen.

"Maria just walked straight into the bedroom while I was in the shower," I whispered.

I don't know why I whispered, as Maria didn't speak any English and was still humming to herself anyway. Nick found it hilarious, but less than 24 hours since we had arrived, I was less than impressed with all our visitors.

Nick went to offer Maria a drink but she shook her head and motioned towards a bottle of water that she had brought with her, and continued cleaning the patio doors. I decided to address the issue of her regular visits.

"Dona Maria," I said, trying to get her attention. "Erm, não todos os dias? Not every day?"

"Sim senhora, todos os dias."

"But-," I struggled on with my basic Portuguese. "Não é necessário."

"Sim, é necessário," she waved one arm in the air, indicating all the bedrooms and bathrooms, kitchen, floors, windows that had to be cleaned.

She obviously thought I was expecting her to do it all in less time when I didn't want her to come at all.

"But ... férias?"

"Não senhora, todos os dias."

I wasn't making much progress, I would just have to try again with Terry, so I left Maria to her chores. She had the knack of appearing in whichever room we had settled in, so we decided to go out for breakfast and then do some shopping, hoping she would have gone by the time we got back.

I had attended Portuguese classes at a local night school in the UK, along with my mum and our friend Carol, whose husband was Portuguese. However, we were surprised on the first night to find that our teacher was English. She obviously had a good knowledge of the language but it's not quite the same. She didn't speak at the same speed as a native speaker, so although we had picked up some grammar and vocabulary, mostly relating to restaurants and shops, we hadn't achieved the level of aural comprehension needed now we were living here, or the vocabulary needed to discuss working hours with Maria.

While we were out, we bought two Portuguese mobiles, just cheap pay-as-you-go handsets, but at least we were able to text family back in the UK and call local numbers, without the huge roaming charges which were in force then. We already had bank accounts and knew all about the Multibanco system, which was far in advance of the UK ATM equivalent at the time. You could do everything from a Multibanco machine, including paying bills and topping up mobile phones, which was really useful until you got stuck behind someone with a month's worth of invoices. Cheques were a different matter, you could order them but the banks only supplied 5 or 10 at a time and they had a limited validity, so if you hadn't used them within 6 months, they were worthless.

It was still better than the travel cheques we used to bring on holiday in the 80s and 90s. In those days there was just one bank, facing onto the square. It only opened for a few hours each morning and afternoon, with a 2-hour lunch break in the middle, and therefore had a permanent queue of tourists waiting to collect their escudos. It was always a thought to have to go and wait in the searing heat, but the one cashier behind the counter treated every customer as if they were the only one he would attend to all day. Each transaction took forever with much filling in of forms and rubber-stamping of duplicate copies. Then he had to count the notes and coins taken from the drawer, then again for himself and a third time for the customer. We rented villas on various developments and had to practice the address for the form. Vale do Milho we could manage, but Areias dos Moinhos was always a struggle and we often resorted to just showing him our booking form to save our blushes at our terrible pronunciation.

We already had our NIF or Fiscal Number, which we had needed when buying our rental apartment a few years earlier, so that made buying the phones easier, and we knew we could top them up at any ATM. A fiscal number is a bit like a UK National Insurance number but used much more widely, and necessary for just about everything, when opening a bank account, renting, buying or selling property, or vehicles, or pretty much anything where you wanted an official invoice or guarantee. It also ensures the shop or supplier is putting the sale through the books and charging IVA (VAT) where applicable. To encourage people to pay for goods legally, including IVA, the government introduced an invoice lottery, with prizes of several thousand euros, or even a car, so every invoice with your fiscal number on it is entered into the lottery. So far, we haven't won a thing! There is another advantage to registering your purchases to your fiscal number; each year when you submit your IRS declaration, the amount you owe is reduced by a percentage of what you've spent in various categories like health, education, car maintenance, hairdressers, veterinary costs etc, and that can mount up over a year.

Getting the phones and having a Portuguese number amounted to another step towards feeling we were really living here now and not just tourists. The next one was to get the internet installed. There was a landline in the villa so we assumed it would be a fairly simple procedure, and I needed internet access for rental clients to be able to book the apartment. I rang Terry and asked how we should go about it.

"Ah, well, that might be a bit tricky," he replied less than enthusiastically.

"Why?" I asked. "There's already a phone line."

"Well, it's in a previous owner's name."

"Ok, so how do we change it?"

"I don't think we'll be able to. You see, she has to go to Portugal Telecom and sign it over to the new owner."

"And doesn't she live locally anymore?"

"Erm, no, she died a few years ago."

"So that's it, no way round it?"

"Well, you could get a new phone line put in, in your name, but that would be pretty expensive and you'd be tied into a 2-year contract."

I sighed in disbelief.

"So, this phone line can never be changed or cancelled?"

"Well, if we could find a relative of the previous owner, or their solicitor, and they could provide a copy of a death certificate..." he tailed off, realising he wasn't really helping.

We were only going to be staying here for 6 months, as the owners already had bookings for next spring and summer. It certainly wasn't worth our while to go looking for death certificates from who knows when, or paying for a whole new phone line and internet installation. We'd have to find another solution, and quickly.

Maria continued to arrive by 9 am, every day. We might as well have been going to work, having to be up, showered and dressed before she arrived, as she still had no concept of personal space. She jealously guarded her chores and if she caught us washing up, she would sidle up to us, ostensibly 'helping' by drying and putting away the dishes, but in reality, she edged closer and closer until we had to give in and walk away and allow her free access to the soapy water. She even wanted to do our laundry. The washing machine was locked in a cupboard off the kitchen and only Maria had the key. When I asked if she would open it for me, she shook her head.

"Muito complicado," she said, obviously believing me incapable of pressing a few buttons.

I really had to draw the line at this, there was no way that Maria was going to be washing our smalls. After a few conversations with Terry, eventually, I won this particular battle and the room was left open at all times, but I could tell she did it under sufferance and I never dared use the machine in Maria's presence. She did take any opportunity to bring the washing in if I wasn't quick enough, and iron it, every single last piece, with a slightly smug look on her face.

Our little feline neighbour grew braver and had started climbing onto the balcony to be fed. She was so pretty and so determined to get closer to us. We left food out every evening, then made sure the patio doors were shut and the dogs inside, so they didn't scare her away. One morning, we found her curled up inside a flower pot and so the balcony became her territory and we made her a bed from an old cushion, and a woolly hat I had used for dog walks in the UK but had no need for now. We named her Catkin and soon she knew her name and came when we called.

A few weeks passed and one day she appeared trailing two young kittens behind her, one ginger and one grey tabby. They were much more nervous and wouldn't come onto the balcony when we were there, but we watched them follow Catkin and started leaving out enough food for the three of them. The kittens looked so small and thin, and we assumed Catkin was their mother. They gulped the food down in a few mouthfuls and would have eaten more except Catkin gave them a smack if they got too close to her rations.

Our other regular visitor was Fernando, who looked after the garden and cleaned and maintained the swimming pool, although it was too cold for us to use it now. He arrived every Wednesday and Saturday morning, always cheerful and ready for a chat, ignoring the fact that he didn't speak or understand one word of English. Nick had only a rudimentary knowledge of Portuguese but somehow, with a lot of mime and the odd word that he did know, they managed to have reasonable conversations. Nick would come in to tell me that Fernando lived near the big supermarket on the edge of the village, or that he grew favas, that is beans, on his piece of land. He had a wife but no children and his wife had a flock of chickens for eggs and also for the pot. Over the weeks, their chats grew longer and more informative, as Fernando showed Nick around the garden and explained about all the plants and how he cared for them. He was a small man, about 8 stone wet through and should probably have retired by now, but he was as devoted to the upkeep of the garden as Maria was to the cleanliness of the house. He travelled everywhere by bicycle, wearing his flat cap and we would often see him cycle past on a Sunday morning, balancing a fishing rod across the handlebars and returning in the late afternoon, usually with a couple of fish for that night's dinner.

We fell into a routine; I still didn't like Maria's continual presence but eventually, I learned to live with it. She, in turn, had become more friendly and we enjoyed little chats about her family. She had 2 sons now living in Lisbon with their own families and a husband who seemed to have some sort of disability. I assumed this was why she was so keen to make sure she came to work every day, not to risk losing their only income, apart from his very small pension.

We found it easier to have breakfast out on the balcony, as that was the last place she mopped and swept before leaving. So that way we gave her free rein to clean and tidy the rest of the house with us safely out of her way. The balcony overlooked the very steep dirt track and not many people passed by as we sat out in the sun, except for one. Almost every morning a young woman walked down the lane in front of the house, heading for the village, accompanied by the most gorgeous dog. He was dark brown with a long, shaggy coat and appeared permanently happy. He was also extremely well-behaved and although she carried a lead, I never saw her put him on it. Compared to our helium dog, he seemed the most perfect example of man's and woman's best friend.

As our next rather overdue priority, we needed to get the car fixed. Nick asked around and the villagers directed him to a local mechanic, Carlos, who spoke perfect English and thankfully, within a few days, the car agreed to fire on all cylinders.

7

Company

Approximately a month after our arrival, my parents took the leap and moved to Portugal. They had already bought a property and early one November afternoon, they flew in with their two dogs as cargo on the plane and we headed off to the airport to pick them up. The flight landed on time and we met mum and dad at arrivals, then drove around to what had been the old terminal building from our trips in the 80s and 90s, now transformed into the cargo pick up point. The dogs looked fine, pleased to see us and apparently suffered no ill effects from the short flight, so we all set off to their new home.

Our next visitor to arrive was Clive, a good friend who had agreed to drive our belongings out in his van, accompanied by his teenage daughter, while his wife and teenage son flew over to stay with us, so they could all enjoy a bit of a holiday and help us unload our belongings. We had brought relatively little with us. We sold most of our furniture, knowing we would be renting initially and the style of furniture in our UK property wouldn't really 'go' in an Algarve villa. So, we looked forward to welcoming one transit-van load of clothes and personal possessions, plus our wrought iron, Victorian bedstead. After living out of a very small suitcase, all we had had space for in the roof box, I was very glad to see the rest of my wardrobe. With three spare bedrooms, the villa offered plenty of space for all our boxes and we enjoyed a fun week with our friends, a little reminder of 'home'.

However, when they went home, I noticed Nick seemed quite down. He had left behind his mum, who was on her own as his dad had died a few years before, two brothers and a wide circle of friends; whereas my sister, Anne-Marie and her partner Steve had already moved to Carvoeiro in the summer, followed shortly by my parents. Nick had been born and raised in the small village we had just left and regularly played golf every Sunday morning with up to a dozen mates. They also took off on an annual golf trip, usually to France. We had been involved from the beginning as I spoke passable French and at that time, pre-internet, all the arrangements for the hotel and golf bookings had to be made by phone, or even fax. Nick had promised to continue going on these golf breaks (never to be called a 'holiday') but the next one wasn't until May. I felt quite happy with my animals, books and just pottering around, but I knew Nick needed to be active. He was used to working 6 days a week in charge of our metal finishing business and he just couldn't get used to having nothing to do all day.

We solved the internet problem by buying a modem. No unlimited access or wi-fi existed in those days, just a dial-up connection, which proved not only very slow and unreliable but also quite expensive. However, at least we could post a message on the local chat forum, asking if anyone wanted a golf partner. To my surprise, we got a reply quite quickly, from a guy who owned a villa nearby and who visited every 6-8 weeks, so we made arrangements for them to have a game on his next visit. That gave Nick something to look forward to but he was still quite restless; he had nothing to do around the house, Maria and Fernando had that all sewn up. We couldn't unpack as we'd be moving on in a few months and there are only so many times you can walk the dogs.

We had seen posters go up in the village advertising celebrations for Dia de São Martinho, St Martin's Day, on the 11th November. It has become synonymous with celebrating the harvest with roasted chestnuts and tasting the first wines of the season, usually on the nearest weekend to the actual date.

É dia de São Martinho. Comem-se castanhas; prova-se o vinho!

It's St Martin's Day. Chestnuts are eaten; wine is tasted!

We decided to meet up with Anne-Marie and Steve at this local festival to get to know some Portuguese traditions. Nick absolutely loves roast chestnuts so he was particularly looking forward to it. The morning of the festival broke grey and cloudy but often the sun burnt through the clouds and the weather cleared as the day progressed. Anyway, we had no way of contacting the organisers to check if they were still planning to go ahead, so we started walking down to the square at 12.30 as arranged. If there was no festival we could still meet for a coffee and a chat in one of the cafes. As we made our way down to the square, the clouds grew darker and heavier and as soon as we turned towards the sea, a huge gusting wind blew horizontal rain straight at us. Of course, the square was deserted, with no lovely smell of roasting chestnuts or sound of popping corks, just the wind whipping in off the Atlantic. As we stood on the corner of the street, we spotted two orange cagoules bobbing down the opposite hill. With their hoods up and tightly closed, most people would find it impossible to identify the occupants, unless you knew them as well as we did. Anne-Marie and Steve had also held high hopes of improving conditions and as with us, the weather had caught them out halfway down.

The whole village seemed deserted, obviously, they'd seen more accurate forecasts than we had. We stood in the pelting rain for a few moments, until Nick remembered seeing one cafe open, so we set off for our own wine tasting and the chance to dry off.

The weather rapidly turned cooler, as well as wetter, so we decided to try the central heating, which had been one of our main reasons for renting this villa. It's quite unusual to have central heating in the Algarve and we soon found out why. There's no piped gas in the area, so you have to use the bottled variety. We had seen two large bottles outside the kitchen and asked Maria to demonstrate how to use the system. It bore no resemblance to anything we knew and, pleased to be needed for something, she gladly explained the controls, timer, thermostat etc. With no need for heating during the summer months, we had no idea when it had last been pressed into service, but it didn't seem keen on co-operating. A lot of hissing and gurgling ensued, not to mention an ominous banging. We raced around all the bedrooms and bathrooms, up and down the stairs, but none of the radiators felt any warmer.

Maria tried again, re-setting all the controls and checking the gas connection outside, but the radiators remained stone cold. She gave up with a shrug; we'd have to call Terry and see if he could get it working.

After several attempts, Terry finally answered the phone and I could hear him sucking his teeth as I explained the situation.

"Right, well, erm, the heating *can* be a bit tricky. I'll pop round later and have a look."

No time specified, I wasn't even sure he meant today; 'later' could be more or less anything in Terry's vocabulary. With unreliable, or indeed no central heating, the house felt absolutely freezing. We had loved the glass wall of patio doors during warmer weather, but now the wind whistled straight through the huge gaps between them into a space already too large to heat. Nick turned his attention to the wood burner at the other end of the room, an ancient feature and as with the heating, no one appeared to have used it for a very long time. The door seemed welded shut but after an application of WD40, the handle reluctantly squeaked open revealing an interior three-quarters full of ash. We set to work emptying it out and cleaning the glass in the door, made up of loose strips which slid along channels built into the top and bottom of the door. It didn't seem particularly safe or well-designed for keeping smoke in. We had seen bags of logs and kindling start to appear in the supermarket, so headed off to stock up on everything we'd need for a roaring fire.

When we got back, we discovered a note from Terry on the dining table: 'Heating sorted'.

No instructions followed as to how we could 'sort' it, but the house did feel slightly warmer; perhaps we could make it cosy for the winter after all. We lit the fire, to supplement the heating and the flames did help both with heat and lending the room a more cheerful atmosphere, so we allowed ourselves to relax a little.

The following morning, we awoke to a freezing bedroom. Nick checked the gas bottles and found to his amazement that they were both empty. The heating had been on for about 6 hours max. Another call to Terry, another voicemail message.

"The gas bottles appear to be empty. Do you know if they were full? How do we go about replacing them?"

We decided to take the dogs for a walk, as it felt warmer outside than in and returned an hour or so later to see a truck stacked with gas bottles disappearing down the road. A quick check by the kitchen window, and yes, two new gas bottles had appeared, an envelope attached to one, containing an invoice for 78 euros.

"I guess the others must have been almost empty," said Nick hopefully, "I wonder how long these two will last?"

The heating clicked on at about 6 pm, now we were getting somewhere. Terry had obviously set up a timer and hopefully a thermostat, so we lit a fire again and looked forward to many more warm and cosy evenings.

We were still feeding Catkin and her kittens, plus a few other strays who heard about the food supply on the balcony, so we often had six or seven visitors each evening. Several were completely feral and seemed to live on the open land across from the villa. They all looked absolutely beautiful. Siamese-type cats with varying shades and shapes of brown masks across their eyes, so we nicknamed them Pretty Mask, Light Mask, Dark Mask etc, not particularly imaginative but just so we knew who had been fed and who was trying to get second helpings. Catkin had definitely taken up residence and now rarely left the balcony. I was still concerned about the dogs, but she seemed happy out there, curled up in my old hat.

We had several more visits from friends that autumn, one of which coincided with the Rugby World Cup. Nick, Pete and Roger went down to the local bar at about 8 am as it was opening early to show the final between England and Australia, live from Sydney. Penny, Jo and I surfaced just in time to see the famous Wilkinson drop goal to win the Cup with 26 seconds remaining. We had literally just sat down with breakfast when it happened and stared at each other in complete disbelief. About an hour later, the boys came back, in extremely high spirits, after a full English breakfast washed down with several pints. Roger was particularly jubilant, but then decided he might just need a 'little lie down' and disappeared for several hours.

We looked forward to our first Christmas in the Algarve and my brother Steven booked a flight for Christmas Eve. As his birthday is just before Christmas, we would have a double celebration. Nick had enjoyed seeing our friends and was looking forward to Christmas but still felt quite down, really not like him at all. He was only in his early 40s and had been used to a busy and responsible job; quite simply, he missed it and the constant interaction with different people throughout the day. He didn't feel ready to slow down at all and I could see he needed something to do, something to get up for. He even offered to work for friends who owned a local company, for free, whenever they needed an extra pair of hands, but they thought he was joking and waved the idea away with a laugh. But he was deadly serious and started scouring the local English language newspapers for vacancies or business opportunities.

Even using the heating on a timer, we were going through gas bottles at an alarming rate. The cooker and hot water also worked on gas but the radiators just ate it up. The log fire on its own didn't provide enough heat to reach the whole of the living room, plus it left the bedroom and kitchen icy cold. The next two bottles lasted 4 days, we really couldn't justify spending over 100 euros a week on heating, whilst paying 1000 euros a month in rent. We felt extremely disappointed as it was one of the main reasons we had chosen this villa. Not only was it dilapidated and neglected, but we also had to put up with Maria's continual presence and now it wasn't even warm.

We decided to investigate which bars and restaurants stayed

open in late November and found a small, friendly cocktail bar, within easy walking distance on the way down, although getting back up the hill presented more of a challenge. However, a few caipirinhas made it a whole lot easier. The owners were a German/Swiss couple, who had spent many years working on cruise ships before settling in the Algarve and consequently offered a fairly extensive cocktail menu. Kurt, with his Swiss background, was also an expert at making Rosti and cheese fondue, while Monika took care of the cocktails, wine, port, digestifs, in fact just about any type of alcohol you could imagine. They always had new wines and liqueurs to taste and on quiet evenings, once we'd finished eating, they would pull up a chair and chat away.

The bar quickly became our local and we spent two or three evenings a week there, often joined by my mum and dad, as it was only a short walk for them too. Although in the opposite direction from us, it also involved a steep hike uphill; you just can't get away from the hills here. Sometimes, we enjoyed a special of picanha or black pork which was actually Kurt and Monika's dinner but they always had enough for us, if we fancied it. Other nights we'd have tapas with local cheeses and cured meats, crusty Alentejo bread, olives and tapenade. If Kurt and Monika were having dessert, then that came our way too and gave us a few extra calories to tackle the uphill trek back home. It was warmer than the villa and saved us from attempting to use the cooker, which behaved extremely temperamentally.

One weekend, I decided to bake a cake but the oven temperature varied so much from top to bottom and side to side, that what emerged resembled half burnt biscuit, half barely cooked batter. After that, I gave up and we tended to use just the hob, living on pasta and sauce or basically anything that could be cooked in a saucepan or frying pan.

We found the run-up to Christmas much more subdued than that in the UK, where the shops start belting out Wizzard in September. I didn't fancy risking roasting a turkey in our uncooperative oven so we decided to book restaurants for both Christmas Day and New Year's Eve. However, virtually everywhere we asked, gave the same response:

"We haven't decided whether to open yet, come back in a few weeks."

We were used to Christmas menus appearing at the same time as Hallowe'en parties and with Christmas only a few weeks away, I had expected to be told they were all fully booked, not that they hadn't prepared a menu or started taking bookings. We learnt a lot in our first months here, namely that things happened in their own time, no rush, we'll get there in the end. And so it proved; when one of our favourite restaurants put out a blackboard with their Christmas menu, in the first week of December, we went straight in to book a table. The waiter seemed a bit surprised.

"A provisional booking?" he asked.

"No," I said. "We want to confirm a reservation for lunch on Christmas Day, the 25th."

As we discovered, in Portugal, along with many other European countries, they celebrated the 24th as the most important day and had their Christmas dinner, traditionally of bacalhau, salt cod, late on Christmas Eve and then opened their presents. Most of the bars and restaurants closed on the afternoon of the 24th and everyone gathered for a home-cooked family meal and celebration. We saw plenty of women walking from their house to a family member, each carrying a saucepan or casserole dish wrapped in a tea towel and containing their contribution to the feast. It did make the village very quiet on Christmas Eve, another marked difference to the UK where the pub tills would be ringing all evening. We also noted a distinct lack of decorations. A few went up at the beginning of December, but apparently, some years, if the local council couldn't afford it, none appeared at all.

We were all organised for Steven's visit and planned to do a buffet supper as his flight wasn't due to arrive until the afternoon of Christmas Eve, plus we had our Christmas lunch booked for the following day.

One evening, the cats and kittens all turned up for dinner as usual, but I noticed that the shyest kitten, a grey tabby, had a problem with his eye. It looked swollen and black, no pupil or iris visible and he couldn't seem to close his eyelid. It looked very painful. I called Nick over to check it out.

"That does look nasty," he said. "I think we'll need to get him up to the vet."

Now, how to achieve this? We had never touched any of the cats, they would never come close enough. Suddenly we needed to catch one, obviously in pain, totally feral and we had no idea how to start. We didn't even have a cat box. The next night they came back again, and we rigged up a sturdy cardboard box, with a blanket and some food inside and stepped back behind a pillar, just close enough to attempt to secure the box with a lid and a blanket, should the injured kitten go inside. Ha! Poorly as he was, he had no intention of falling for our trap. He scooped the food out with his paw and disappeared through the wrought iron fence.

We tried again the next night, aware that Christmas was in just a few days, meaning we would have to wait until after all the festivities to get him some treatment. Whether he knew we were trying to help, or was feeling weaker, I don't know, but this time we managed it and quickly headed off to the vet. We hadn't had any reason to visit the clinic before, but we had seen it on our travels, so decided to take a chance and just turn up and throw ourselves, and the kitten, on their mercy. It was now about 5.30 pm and dark and then the heavens opened. I sat in the back seat, trying to keep the box secure while allowing a small gap for fresh air when he suddenly leapt out and jumped into the boot of our hatchback. This took it to an entirely new level. We now had a feral, injured kitten loose in the car, what if he decided to leap onto Nick while he was driving, or creep under the pedals? I screamed in shock, Nick turned around and saw the open box.

"Where is he?"

"I don't know, I think he's in the boot!"

"Well, have a look!"

I took a quick glance but couldn't see him; only when I knelt up on the seat and leant over, did I finally spot him, huddled in a corner. He was quiet and still and looked as though he planned on staying there. The vet was only five minutes away now, fingers crossed he wouldn't decide to start wandering around. When we finally pulled up at the clinic, Nick slid out of the driver's door, only opening it as much as he had to, while I kept the kitten under surveillance. A few minutes later, a young woman vet came out, carrying a towel and a proper cat box. She opened the back door a fraction.

"Where is he?" she whispered.

I pointed and nodded my head towards the boot.

"Ok, I will try," she said and knelt beside me.

I decided it was safer to be outside the car, so I stepped out before she made any attempt to catch him. We watched as she leant over and tried to throw the towel over him, to temporarily disorientate him and allow her to slide him into the box. He suddenly leapt into action and sank his teeth into her arm. He was on alert now, running from side to side, growling, hissing and baring his teeth. With blood dripping down her arm, she valiantly carried on, waiting until he calmed down a little, then made another attempt. We found her calm patience quite incredible. She was as determined to catch him, as he was to evade capture.

We continued standing outside in the rain, not feeling we could go inside and leave her on her own, not that we provided any help at all, but we felt too guilty to just walk away. After about half an hour, we saw a thumbs-up through the steamy window and the door opened. She had him safely in the cat box, still growling and panting heavily. We trudged to the clinic door, a sorry sight, both of us soaked to the skin and the young vet leaving a trail of blood along the path.

Once inside and having cleaned and dressed her wounds, Patricia took a look at the kitten through the grill of the box. She shook her head sadly.

"This eye has a big infection, too big, we will have to remove it."

We both felt shocked. He was so young, and I had expected some antibiotics or other treatment would be able to help him but to have his eye removed?

"This is your cat?" she asked.

"No, he isn't," I replied. "He's a stray but we've been feeding him along with his brother and a few others."

"Ok, leave him with us, we will do the surgery tomorrow but he will need to stay inside for 10 days for the stitches to heal."

Nick and I looked at each other. How on earth would we manage that? We had plenty of spare bedrooms to put him in, but how to stop him from escaping? Would he let us in to feed him and make sure he got all his medication?

"We can try," I shrugged, "but it will be difficult. We're not used to cats; we have two dogs…" I trailed off.

"I'm sure he will be better once the pain stops," Patricia smiled. "And when he comes home, he will be sleepy from the surgery."

Home? Were we his home now? How were the dogs going to take to this new situation?

"Does he have a name?" she asked.

"No, we just call them tabby kitten and ginger kitten."

"I will call him Camões," she said, still smiling. "Do you know what it is? Camões?"

We shook our heads. We'd only been here just over two months and weren't up to speed with Portuguese history and culture.

"Camões is the great poet Luis de Camões, one of the most famous Portuguese writers, and he only had one eye," she winked.

We now felt concerned for the ginger kitten. If he was going to be separated from his brother for 10-12 days, would they remember each other?

The operation went well and we picked Camões up the following day, December 23rd. We were better prepared this time; we had bought a cat box and prepared one of the spare downstairs bedrooms for him. Explaining to Maria was a bit of a trial, trying to mime removing his eye proved interesting. She looked totally perplexed, as if she thought we were going to do it ourselves, but as long as she understood not to go into that bedroom under any circumstances until I told her it was ok, that was the most important part.

We were pleasantly surprised at the cost of the surgery; he had been neutered at the same time and the total price amounted to half what we had expected, based on UK vet prices. The poor boy had a cone of shame on, to make sure he left the stitches alone and must have wondered what on earth had happened to him over the last couple of days.

We arrived home and took him straight to his new bedroom. He complained a bit as he wandered around investigating and bumping into everything as he wasn't used to wearing the cone, and of course, only had one eye. We had closed all the shutters so he wasn't tempted by views of the outdoors and left him to get used to his new quarters in peace. Luckily, he seemed quite happy to take his medication in his food and we had bought some tasty tins of tuna and sardines to encourage him.

That evening, his brother arrived as normal and we managed to catch him quite easily, again thanks to some tempting treats. I carried him into the bedroom to see Camões and they spent a good half an hour inspecting each other and having a good sniff all over. Ginger could obviously smell the clinic, the other animals and the other people he'd been in contact with, but he didn't appear fazed at all and they were soon grooming each other as usual. They seemed so happy to see each other that we decided to take a chance on leaving them together overnight and letting Ginger out in the morning. This worked really well and continued during Camões's convalescence. I'm sure it helped his recovery, having his brother to cuddle up to at night.

Christmas Eve dawned bright and sunny. Steven sent a text to say he was on his way to the airport and the flight looked to be on time, so we started getting ready to host the celebrations. No cleaning to do and for once I was glad of Maria and her attention to detail, so we took a quick trip to the supermarket. None of the huge queues had formed, that you get in the UK so close to Christmas; in fact, it could have been a normal day. As we arrived back at the villa, my phone beeped,

'Looks like an hour delay, speak soon, S'

"Okaaaaay," I said. "An hour, that's not too bad, he was due to land at 4.30 in Faro. He should still be here by 6.30 or so."

We continued our preparations, laying the table with the best china and cutlery that the villa had to offer and some decorations that we had bought to try to cheer the place up a bit. Beep!

'Another hour delay, speak soon, S'

"So, 7.30?" I said, optimistically. "Still time to eat and have a few drinks."

Beep!

'Flight no longer on screen, will try airport information, speak later, S'

Now, this was a worrying development. Not expecting to spend Christmas in his flat, Steven would have emptied the fridge and everywhere would be starting to close. Would he even find any public transport running to take him back to London?

I cranked up our dial-up modem to check the Gatwick flights; no information there either. What a nightmare. Beep!

'Flight's back up, but just says delayed, speak soon, S'

What did that mean? Was it coming or not? When would the airport shut down? Would there be any flights on Christmas Day?

Mum and Dad, Anne-Marie and Steve arrived, with their contributions of food and drinks, so we carried on preparing the food for the buffet but with much less enthusiasm now and a low, insistent nag of panic. Beep!

'Gate's open, boarding, see you soon, S'

I had to read it 3 or 4 times, then showed it to Nick,

"It says he's boarding!"

"Great," he said. "What time will I need to pick him up?"

We didn't actually know when the flight was taking off, Steven had switched his phone off and Faro's website denied all knowledge of a Gatwick flight. It took around 45 minutes to get there, so we couldn't hang around waiting for information. We made a rough calculation of take-off and flight time.

"I don't think they'll land until about 10.30," said Nick. "I'll have to leave just after 9.30."

Slap bang in the middle of the evening, I thought. Nothing else for it, the rest of us would have to make a start on the food and hope that it wouldn't be too late before the boys got back. Just after Nick left, the Faro arrivals board finally showed the incoming flight, due at 10.45. Fortunately, the airport would be quiet and we hoped he would get through quickly.

Beep!

'In car, on way, see you soon, S'

Thank goodness for that, it was just after 11. We re-arranged the plates of food to hide the gaps where we had tucked into the buffet and made sure the fridge had plenty of cold beers at the ready. Finally, the car headlights swept up the drive at 5 to midnight. Happy Christmas!

8

New Year's Resolutions

We had a great week. Christmas Day dawned bright and beautiful and after lunch, we enjoyed a long walk along the deserted beach. Although we had visited in winter before, we had never spent Christmas here and it proved quite an eye-opener. We hadn't expected the weather to be just as good in the daytime, with temperatures still in the late teens to early twenties, but by the time the sun went down, it could drop 10 degrees in an hour. We quickly learnt to get the house and ourselves prepared for the cool evenings, while the sun still shone and had the fire lit well in advance by 5 pm. We also pulled on socks and jumpers, as once we got cold, we found it really hard to warm up again. However, I loved having the different seasons; I don't think I would have enjoyed living somewhere with the same climate all year round. We could look forward to salads and long summer evenings, but also enjoy the winter, with the cosiness of log fires and warming soups and stews.

For Steven, it was a revelation to sit in the sun with a cold beer in December and he developed a love for the Algarve in that week.

The time soon came for his return trip to Faro, a less eventful one this time, and for us to prepare for New Year's Eve. It was much livelier than Christmas Eve, with lots of restaurants and bars open until 2 or 3 am, many serving caldo verde soup as an early breakfast, just before the end of the partying. We also learned the custom of eating 12 raisins, one with each stroke of midnight bringing good luck for each of the coming 12 months. Waiters in the restaurants brought out dishes, or small bags, of raisins to every table, usually along with a glass of bubbly to toast the New Year. Then everyone went outside to make as much noise as possible, beeping car horns, or bashing saucepans together from a balcony, traditionally to chase off evil spirits.

New Year's Day remained a quiet one, similar to the UK, with everyone recovering from a late night of drinking and dancing, although some brave souls insisted on a swim in the sea to clear their heads.

In Portugal, we discovered that if a bank holiday fell on a weekend, there was no day off in lieu, so if Christmas Day and New Year's Day fell on a Saturday or Sunday it meant back to work on Monday, not even a Boxing Day in between. This could result in a normal working week, sandwiched between two busy weekends. As we were used to a 10 - 14 day shutdown, it came as a bit of a shock to have two distinct holidays rather than one extended one. It did mean that life continued as normal and we could take Camões for a check-up on the 2nd of January. His eye had healed up really well and they gave us permission to remove the cone of shame and let him out again. I felt so relieved; I'd worried about his recovery, now we had to just wait to see how he'd cope with only one eye.

With Christmas and New Year over, Nick slid back into a slump. He just couldn't get used to the lack of structure and feeling of uselessness caused by our situation. He couldn't even busy himself with DIY or gardening; we didn't own the house so it wasn't our responsibility to maintain, although goodness knows it needed it. We had never lived in a rented property before so this was all new to both of us, and knowing our stay would only last for 6 months gave us a feeling of instability which didn't help his mood.

"I've been looking through the local papers," he announced one morning, "looking for vacancies or business opportunities."

"Oh, yes?" I replied, already wary of whatever scheme he might have dreamt up.

"I don't see anyone offering a man with a van service."

"Ok, do we need a man with a van?"

"No, for me, I could be a man with a van."

I looked up.

"But you don't have a van?"

"Well, I could get one."

"Yeeees, you could, but wouldn't it be expensive?"

"Well, a second-hand one shouldn't be too much."

"But it also might not be very reliable?"

I could see our little nest egg dwindling fast at this rate, paying rent and now buying a van and we still had to buy a house at some stage.

"Hmmm."

I could tell he was still keen on the idea, and not so keen on my objections, which I thought perfectly reasonable.

"If there isn't anyone already doing it, how do you know there's a market for a man with a van?" I asked.

"Well, I could put an advert in the English language papers."

"And what if you get any work? And you don't have a van?"

"I'll hire one," he said triumphantly.

"But then you won't make any money."

"Maybe not to start with, but if I get enough enquiries, then I'll buy a van. It's got to be worth speculating a few euros on an advert to find out."

He definitely wasn't giving up, so we drafted a short ad,

including his new Portuguese mobile number and waited for publication.

The following weekend, we decided to take a trip to the nearest shopping centre, with its wide variety of shops, a cinema and a food court. We queued up at a pasta place, deciding which sauce and ingredients to go with our tagliatelle when Nick's phone rang. We looked at each other in surprise, it wasn't a number we recognised.

"Answer it quick, it might be a response to your ad," I whispered. "Just tell me what you want on your pasta!"

"Anything, you choose," he replied and wandered off to a quieter area with the phone to his ear.

I watched the back of his head nodding; then I heard him talking, although frustratingly I couldn't hear a word. I ordered lunch, still watching Nick and trying to work out if it was an enquiry about a job. He turned around, beaming.

"That was a guy needing a small house removal. I told him I've got a lot on and have to move things around, so that will give me time to find a van and I'll ring him later to arrange a day and time."

"Wow! So, the ad worked?"

"Yes, he said he'd been looking for someone to help him for a while. Quick, let's finish lunch and get back so I can start looking for a van."

Within a few hours, he had arranged to hire a van and agreed a day for the removal. Next, we had to make it official and register with the local Finanças. As we discovered, each town in Portugal had its own tax office, rather than a centralised system like in the U.K. You went in person, took a 'senha' or ticket for the relevant department and waited for your number to be called. It could be a few minutes or several hours, you never knew. If you had the bad luck to get a high numbered ticket, you went off for a coffee or stood outside chatting, popping your head in now and again to see how far the queue had moved. Nick was in luck, not many people wanted to open an activity, as they called it and he completed the process in half an hour. We had achieved our first real bit of Portuguese bureaucracy.

Now he was registered to work, we had to sort out residency, social security, an accountant, exchange our UK driving licences; the list seemed endless and extremely daunting, so we decided to employ an agency to help us negotiate the various systems. We made an appointment for the following day and they gave us a list of documents to bring with us.

We turned up to meet Susie, a fast-talking Brazilian woman, who sat at a desk surrounded by piles and piles of papers. She fished around and found an empty file, wrote our names on the front and started filling it with too many forms to count. As she worked, she explained each one in rapid succession.

"This we need for the driving licence," she looked up. "You bring your English licence?"

We nodded.

"Hm, you have fiscal numbers?"

We nodded again.

"Good."

This went on for about half an hour, Susie firing questions and us nodding along. She never left a space for us to reply.

"Sign here and here and this one."

She placed a series of forms in front of us, indicating with a long, brightly painted fingernail where we should sign, then swopping the papers between us, flipping them over in a mesmerising and well-rehearsed routine. We felt completely lost but finally, she closed the file and sat back.

"I will make appointments with SEF for the residencia, with IMT for the driving licence and will apply for social security numbers for you. I will call to tell you when we go. Ok?"

We nodded again, she had dismissed us, politely but firmly and we stumbled out in a bit of a daze. The next clients waited nervously, shuffling all their vital documents, checking they hadn't forgotten anything. I knew exactly how they felt and gave them what I hoped was a reassuring smile. Susie appeared behind us.

"Next clients please!"

The following week involved a whirlwind of visits to different government offices, Susie marching ahead as we trailed in her wake. We became the subject of many discussions, photographed and fingerprinted, but finally, we had everything we needed to be legal Portuguese residents, or at least pieces of paper that would serve as proof until the new residence cards and licences were issued. We had paid for Susie's help but thought it money well spent as we would have struggled to get so much done in such a short time on our own. Nick also completed his removal job, losing about 100 euros on the deal, but he'd proved that the service was needed and received several more enquiries. So off he set to look for a van.

With his new business plan in place, Nick felt much more

positive. He had also met up with the other Nick, who had replied to my plea for a golf buddy and they enjoyed a great round of golf, followed by a few beers. This became a regular thing every time 'golf Nick' and his wife came to stay in their villa, just a few minutes drive from our house and they remain our friends to this day, almost 20 years later. My Nick also had a visit from his mum to look forward to, the first time she had been to Portugal. She came for a week that January and promptly fell in love with the place too. Having spent many years in Italy and Germany whilst Nick's dad worked on the Tornado aircraft project, she had come to enjoy the pavement cafe lifestyle, which Carvoeiro also offered. She even said that she wished she'd visited earlier as she may well have moved over too, but at 75 she felt she'd left it too late.

However, once back home she soon made plans to return. She started by renting an apartment for 4-6 weeks at a time, spending spring and autumn in Portugal and even a month at Christmas. Every morning, she walked the couple of hundred metres to Smilers bar, stopping to buy a newspaper on the way. Once seated, always at the same corner table for maximum people-watching opportunities, she completed the crossword and caught up on the news, accompanied by a galão, a milky coffee served in a tall glass. Some days, she would still be there at lunchtime when she'd treat herself to a glass of wine or gin and tonic before heading back to the apartment for an afternoon on the balcony with a good book.

Her visits continued for around 10 years until the travelling became too much of a trial and she reluctantly stopped. However, she kept a soft spot for Portugal in her heart and loved to hear any local news during Nick's weekly phone calls, or his regular visits until sadly she died in 2020.

I felt quite happy pottering around and managing the bookings for our apartment, not really looking for a job until one day I saw an advertisement in the local paper for an estate agent in the village; it didn't mention which one. I applied on a whim, intrigued to know which of the many agents it referred to and whether or not I stood a chance of getting the job. A few days later, I was surprised to receive a phone call inviting me for an interview. I went along, knowing I probably wouldn't be successful and not even sure if I wanted the job. The advert concerned a full-time position, but I only really wanted to work part-time. The office stood right in the middle of the village and represented one of the longest-established agents. We had often walked past on previous holidays and stopped to daydream about buying a place, never thinking that we would ever make the move. Now I found myself as a potential employee, it felt quite surreal.

A fairly informal, chatty interview ensued and I thought I could quite enjoy the work but didn't pick up any clues as to how I'd done.

I arrived back at the villa, keen to tell Nick all about it but he appeared clearly distracted.

"How was your shower this morning?"

"Erm, wet? I thought you were going to ask how was the interview?"

"Oh yes, how was it?" he muttered, as he left one bathroom and headed for another.

"Fine, I don't know if I'll get it but-,"

"Was it hot?" he interrupted.

"The interview?"

"The shower, was it hot?"

"Oh, I don't really remember, it must have been ok. It was at Edward's, you know, the shop with windows onto the in road and the out road?"

But he was off again, towards the kitchen this time.

"Are you listening?" not for the first time in our relationship had I asked that question.

"I can't get any hot water out of any of the taps," he replied.

So, I guessed he wasn't listening.

This villa had rapidly turned into a nightmare. The cold, the damp, the statues and now no hot water. We reported the problem and a plumber turned up a few hours later. Paulo was about 30, spoke excellent English and knew his way around the house. Obviously, problems had occurred before. After about half an hour of checking the kitchen and bathrooms, squeezing into the cupboard under the sink, then into the laundry room containing the boiler, he emerged.

"I'm sorry, I don't find the problem," he shrugged. "Everything works ok."

"But we still don't have any hot water!" Nick almost exploded. "What are we supposed to do?"

"I will come back tomorrow with a colleague and look more."

We looked at each other in despair, the nights had turned really cold now and only freezing water emerged from both hot and cold taps. We couldn't possibly take a shower in the morning.

"I come tomorrow, 100 per cent," promised Paulo, disappearing out of the front door before we could question him further.

Just as we had started to make some progress, this came as a considerable step backwards; we would have to wait until Paulo and his colleague returned and sensed it wouldn't be an easy fix.

"Thank goodness it didn't happen while your mum was here," I said; the only consolation I could offer.

"Yes, let's be grateful for small mercies," replied Nick. "But if it was the summer, at least we could have had a swim."

The next morning, I couldn't bear it and took the quickest shower on record, my teeth were actually chattering as I wrapped myself in a huge towel and got back under the covers to warm up a bit. I didn't even care when Maria came in to sweep and mop the floor, just grunted: "Bom dia," and stayed in my cocoon until I started to feel my feet again.

Paulo arrived at 10.30, a fairly usual time for workmen to turn up, following a leisurely breakfast at their favourite cafe. His colleague was much older, with a large moustache and a flat cap worn down over his forehead making it hard to tell what he looked like. I certainly wouldn't have been able to pick him out of a line-up. We left them to it and took the dogs for a walk, hoping for a miracle.

We returned to a hive of activity; Paulo driving a small digger gouging a channel in the gravel around the house and his colleague sinking a hole in the garden under the front balcony. We stopped, completely stunned.

"Erm, what's- erm, what are you- erm-?"

Nick couldn't even get the words out and Paulo couldn't hear him anyway, over the noise of the machine. Nick took a few steps closer and waved vaguely in his line of vision.

"Sorry Mr Nick, I don't see you. Sorry, we have a problem."

"Yes, I can see that."

"Yes," he said, looking down, not wishing to make eye contact. "We have a big problem - with the water."

"Yes, we have no hot water, I know."

"No Mr Nick, we have no water."

This shocked us into silence. I was ready to burst into tears, I'd had enough of this dump.

He had dug the trench, in an attempt to see if the water was escaping anywhere underground. Apparently, the pressure had been dropping, which meant the boiler hadn't been firing up and while we were out, it had slowed to a trickle and stopped altogether.

"So, what do we do now?" asked Nick.

"We try to find where the water escapes. The pipes arrive there," replied Paulo, gesturing to the hole in the drive. "And in this pipe is water, but in the house, no water."

They carried on working for the rest of the day, adding a blue dye to the water from the mains and trying to see if they could trace it to an underground leak, but it remained elusive.

This time I was the one on a downward spiral. I threw myself on the bed and turned to the wall. We relied on the owners and the manager to resolve the situation. As it wasn't our house, we weren't in control of the investigations or any repairs required. We could refuse to pay the rent, but that wasn't due for another 3 weeks. Surely, they would sort it by then?

Nick walked in.

"Come on, let's go."

"Where?" I replied. "It's 6 o'clock, it's dark and cold, just where are we going?"

He started pulling clothes out of the wardrobe and toiletries from the bathroom.

"You go and get the dog food and bowls," he said. "Feed the cats and I'll pack what we need. We'll have to go to the apartment; thank goodness it's empty, we can at least have a shower and sleep there while they sort this mess out."

It hadn't even occurred to me that we could go to our place; it wasn't ideal for the dogs but for a few days we could manage. We loaded the car, added some logs and firefighters, as the apartment had stayed empty for a few weeks and we'd need to warm the place up. We left the villa in darkness. I was beginning to hate the sight of the place.

The apartment covered the 3rd and 4th floors of the building, with a tiny square lift. We could only fit one person and one dog in at a time, so I went on up with Gem and Nick followed with Samson, then made a 3rd trip for our few bags of essentials. I lit the fire then started to unpack, heading upstairs to the bedrooms and bathrooms. Our next problem quickly became apparent, Gem was too old and arthritic to manage the wooden stairs and Samson just too skittish. They had managed ok in our old house in England because the stairs had carpet, but these proved too slippery for either of them. They both sat at the bottom, whining. No way could we manhandle them both up and downstairs. Nothing else for it, we brought down the folding bed we kept for extra clients. Nick took that and I slept on the sofa. Thankfully, we had a downstairs cloakroom; so, we set up camp in the living room and grabbed what sleep we could. Surely it wouldn't be for too long.

The next day, Nick popped up to the villa and returned grim-faced.

"They're still no nearer finding out where the leak is."

"You're joking?"

"No, 'fraid not," he sighed. "It looks like it's going to be a major job; they're talking about re-plumbing the whole house."

"I don't believe it, four bathrooms, kitchen and utility? We can't possibly live there while they do all that!"

"No, I know. We'll either have to stay here or look for somewhere else."

"It was hard enough finding that wreck of a place; there are not many places that will take two dogs and we've got the cats to consider now too."

We really had hit a low point. Barely at the end of January and we had signed for the villa until the beginning of April. They had holiday clients due in from Easter. Plus, the village attracted a lot of snowbirds from Canada and Northern Europe, from January to March, so suitable accommodation could be booked up a year in advance. Nick picked up a copy of the local paper and found a few properties available to rent, so we decided we had nothing to lose in arranging a few viewings.

The first place we contacted was empty and pet friendly, the owner seemed keen to rent it and suggested we meet that afternoon. It was an apartment, located right in the centre of the village but up a lot of steps. I made it up with difficulty and decided to take it as a positive; my fitness levels would increase very quickly. A middle-aged Portuguese woman waited for us at the top and ushered us into the darkest hallway I'd ever seen. The building was built into the rock face so only possessed windows on one side. Not only was there a lack of daylight, but the view also consisted of the back of another apartment building and we noticed a distinct smell of damp. I didn't feel at all sure that this place would be an improvement, with or without running water.

We stepped outside into the 'garden', roughly 3 square metres of knee-high weeds, with a few old bricks and broken patio furniture. We also discovered a different smell, not damp this time, but definitely unpleasant. I took a step towards the corner of the building and let out an involuntary cry. The neighbouring garden was full of ducks and turkeys, the stench was unbearable. I rushed back inside, signalling to Nick to follow quickly and made our excuses, that we had other places to view and would be in touch in a few days and reached fresh air in record time.

"Well, that's a non-starter," I whispered, in case we could still be overheard.

"Yes, it was very dark and damp," agreed Nick.

"Not to mention the poultry farm next door."

"What?"

"I didn't think you'd seen it; that was the horrendous smell in the garden."

"Oh, I wondered where that was coming from."

We took the stairs more slowly going down. This had seemed the most promising of the places available. I couldn't face any more viewings; we'd just have to put up with the apartment.

Nick checked on the villa most days but nothing much seemed to be happening and most of the time the place looked completely deserted, except for the cats who still occupied the balcony, undisturbed. So, he made sure they had plenty of food and warm beds. We made calls that were never answered nor returned; neither Paulo nor Terry ever contacted us. It was just getting ridiculous.

We didn't pay the next month's rent. Why should we when we weren't living there? A few days after it was due, surprise, surprise, the phone rang. Nick recognised the number, it was Terry, so he put him on loudspeaker.

"I've got some good news," he started, no apology or mention of the inconvenience but we were keen to find out what glad tidings he was bringing.

"We've spoken to the owners and the quickest way to sort this is to re-plumb the villa."

We both sighed loudly.

"I know, I know," he ploughed on. "But this will be quick, a few days, a week at most. We'll have five or six guys working on it and instead of chasing the pipe work in and re-tiling, we'll just go over the top."

"You mean surface mount all the pipework?" asked Nick.

"Yeah, you've got it, it'll be a doddle."

We stared at each other doubtfully. It would look hideous

but then it wasn't our house and we couldn't carry on the way we were.

"The guys are starting early tomorrow and will stay until six or seven every day until it's finished. They'll get the kitchen and en-suite done first, then you can move back in while they finish the rest."

"Ok, I'll call in tomorrow and have a chat with Paulo," said Nick.

"Champion, all sorted, I knew we'd get there," Terry sounded triumphant. "And as a gesture of goodwill, we'll forget this month's rent. That ok with you?"

"Er, yes, thanks," stumbled Nick, thinking it would at least go some way to making up for all the hassle. "Bye then."

At ten o'clock the next morning, we arrived at the villa to find a hive of activity. Piles of pipes lay dotted around the garden and several trucks stood parked out on the road. The sound of banging and drilling deafened us and echoed dreadfully around the tiled rooms. I wasn't sure about moving back in while they were working but they had made a start.

As we left, my mobile buzzed and I answered without checking the number.

"Hi, this is Edward from the estate agent; you came for an interview a few weeks ago?"

With all the problems at the house, I had completely forgotten about the job.

"Oh, yes, hello."

"I was wondering if you'd like to pop in for another chat. Are you free this afternoon, or tomorrow?"

"Yes, this afternoon would be fine. What time?"

"About 3, is that ok?"

"Yes, absolutely, thank you. See you later."

I felt a bit shocked.

"Nick, hang on a minute," I called as he strode off down the hill. "That was the estate agent, he wants to see me this afternoon!"

"Oh, well done. Maybe he'll offer you the job?"

"Maybe, although I'm still not 100% sure I want it."

"Well, just go with an open mind and see what he's got to say."

I turned up at 3 pm as agreed; it was just a few hundred metres from the apartment and not much further from the villa, not a difficult commute. I saw Edward rushing along the road towards me, an ancient briefcase in one hand and a file of papers in the other. He struggled to fish the keys out of the pocket of his cords and open the door, without his paperwork cascading over the floor.

"Come in, come in, lovely to see you again," he said, hurriedly dumping everything on his desk and turning to shake my hand. "How are you? Well, I hope?"

"Yes, thank you, very well."

"Take a seat, here," he said, dragging a chair from another desk and setting it opposite his.

"So, I've seen a few other candidates, but to be honest, personally," he hesitated a moment, playing with his pen, "I think you'd be a good fit here. What do you think?"

"I think I would enjoy the work, but as I mentioned before, I would only really want to work part-time. Would that be ok?"

Edward leaned back in his chair.

"I've given it some thought and spoken to Elaine, who is here full time at the moment and actually it might be better. We decided we don't really need another full-time person. I advertised for a full-time post as I thought that's what prospective applicants would prefer. So, do you want to give it a try, a couple of weeks to see how we get on? How does three days a week sound?"

It sounded great. I would still manage to look after the apartment rentals and have some time to myself.

"Yes, that sounds good, thanks," I smiled.

"Fantastic, welcome to the team, when do you want to start? Monday? Then Wednesday and Friday?"

"Thank you, yes that's fine. I'm looking forward to it. Erm, there's just one thing, we haven't discussed the salary?"

"Oh, gosh, haven't we? Oh."

Edward seemed a bit flustered and started fiddling with his pen again. He searched through a drawer and pulled out a tiny calculator, then patted his shirt and trouser pockets looking for his glasses. After removing them from the top of his head, he started tapping away and scribbling figures on a piece of paper.

"Here, I think that's right. I'll check with the accountant but it's there or thereabouts."

He passed the paper to me and at the bottom, I saw a figure circled and underlined several times. However, it didn't say if it was weekly, monthly or even annually and I didn't like to ask.

Oh well, I guessed I'd find out.

"Oh, and there will be commission too," he added. "For any properties you sell."

"Ok, thanks, that's good to know," I smiled again.

I felt quite pleased with myself. I'd got the first job I'd applied for, with hours that suited me and any earnings seemed like a bonus for now. It's all experience, I told myself, nothing learnt is ever wasted. We said our goodbyes and I left the office with quite a spring in my step. Things were happening at the villa and I had a new job starting Monday.

I quite looked forward to showing properties to prospective buyers. I always found it interesting to see inside other people's houses and you never know, maybe we'd find something we wanted to buy. A thought suddenly struck me, I was going to have to take clients out, I would have to drive them around or have them follow me. I had never driven a left-hand drive car before, on, to me, the wrong side of the road.

Back at the apartment, I gave Nick the good news.

"I got the job; start Monday and he's agreed to three days a week."

"Brilliant, that's great. Did you ask about the money?"

"Yes, he wrote it down," I replied, passing Nick the scrap of paper.

"This figure at the bottom?"

"Yes."

"What does it mean? Surely not enough for monthly… but too much for weekly?" he said, looking up at me, confused.

"I know, I don't know which it is either. Maybe hourly?" I couldn't resist.

"Yeah right, I'm afraid I think it might be monthly."

And monthly it turned out to be. This was our first real experience of working for a company in Portugal and stupidly, we hadn't researched the average salary. In 2004, the minimum wage was just 425€ per month, full time, so my salary should have been 255€ per month. Edward had in fact been generous and offered me 100€ more than he needed to but it still seemed a paltry sum compared to what we had been used to in the UK and it came as a bit of a shock. Of course, it involved sales commission, depending on how successful I proved and under Portuguese law, employees were entitled to 14 months' salary per year with an extra month paid in August and December for holiday and Christmas expenses. With the tax deductions for amounts spent on things such as health care and education, you could possibly expect to get a refund at the end of the tax year, depending on your circumstances.

"One more thing, Nick."

"Yeah?"

"I need to learn to drive on the other side of the road."

9

Back to Work

We had bought a left-hand drive VW Golf for our trip down to Portugal and at that time, you could matriculate one car each, tax-free, when you moved to Portugal. So, we had the right car, all legal and ready to go, I just hadn't had the courage to drive it. It felt so strange getting in the opposite side and changing gear with my right hand, more than once I almost opened the car door trying to go from first to second. As I had done when first learning to drive twenty years previously, we drove to deserted car parks after the shops had closed to practice the basics, then moved on to reversing into parking spaces. It took several attempts to feel even vaguely comfortable but once I was out of the car parks and onto the roads, I still had a mental block about roundabouts, which resulted in a couple of near misses.

I didn't think I'd be showing clients around on my first day, so decided to just keep practising when I could. When Edward was ready to let me loose on prospective buyers, a few weeks later, he made me drive him around for an hour, just to make sure I was up to it.

The work was progressing on the villa, although we decided not to move back in until it was completely finished. Maria still appeared every day, sweeping and mopping, trying to hold back the tide but the next day it looked as bad as ever. So much dust and noise assaulted us every time we checked on it, that we felt glad to get back to the peace and quiet of the apartment. Finally, a date was set for us to move back in, the Saturday after my first week at work.

I felt really quite nervous as I arrived for my first day at work. We had run our own business before leaving the UK, so a long time had elapsed since I'd worked for someone else. I wasn't sure if I would be able to defer to a boss and take instructions but I needn't have worried, both Edward and Elaine turned out to be friendly and welcoming.

I took my place at my desk. Elaine and I spent the morning going through the lists of properties for sale and then the files of properties 'under offer' and in the process of being sold, while Edward answered calls and dealt with clients making enquiries. The keys for most of the properties hung in a locked cupboard, but for some, we had to contact the house managers, so that gave me another list to familiarise myself with. Having been through the process once, I knew a little of how it worked but would need to improve my knowledge substantially if I was to advise prospective buyers and sellers.

As I discovered, in Portugal at that time, the owner of a property held all the documents, making it easy to see if everything was fully legal, registered at the tax department and local council. When an offer got accepted, those documents were passed to the buyer's lawyer and providing all was in order, they expected the buyer to sign a promissory contract and pay a deposit, usually 10% of the purchase price. This could happen very quickly and take buyers by surprise, especially when used to buying and selling in England. It seemed unnerving and a little scary to be handing over substantial amounts of money within a few weeks of making an offer. Once the promissory was signed, the sale was confirmed. If the buyer changed his or her mind, they lost the deposit. If the seller pulled out, they had to hand over double the amount.

They arranged the completion date to suit all parties, in a few weeks or months, or even a year if everyone agreed. On the day, the buyer and seller, or their representatives if they'd given power of attorney to their lawyer, for example, met at the notary's office to hear the contract *escritura* read out, translated if required, and the parties signed. If the property was mortgaged, a representative from the bank also attended to receive a bank draft to clear the outstanding debt. The seller received their bank draft, the keys were handed over and the sale completed. It took a while to get used to it, but it turned out to be a much simpler way to buy and sell property, with no chance of being gazumped or having similar problems.

I really enjoyed my first day, I learnt a lot just by listening and watching and I could tell that Edward was a popular member of the community by the number of people who popped in for a chat or to arrange a lunch with him. Also, from our position right in the middle of the village, we could see everything that happened on both the 'in' and 'out' roads. With all the people passing by, stopping to look at the villas and apartments displayed in the windows, I found it difficult to tell the serious buyers from the window shoppers at first, but I soon picked up the signs.

My arrival coincided with peak selling time. In general, the clients who came out off-season, and who made contact and appointments in advance, were ready to buy. In summer, we received more tentative enquiries, with visitors seduced by the idea of having a holiday home or making a permanent move, but we often heard nothing more once they returned home.

Between my three days at work and the other two spent preparing to leave the apartment and move back into the villa, I had a busy week. With no time to go to the local supermarket, just picking up fresh rolls from the grocery opposite, I had quite a surprise when we went shopping that Saturday morning. The first aisle as we entered the supermarket appeared full of fancy dress costumes. I picked up a leaflet advertising the outfits and saw 'Carnaval' splashed across the front.

Slowly it dawned on me as I noted the date on the leaflet. I was used to the idea of Carnival in Brazil but hadn't realised that our Shrove Tuesday, or Pancake Day, was also celebrated in Portugal as Carnaval. Although not an official holiday, most places closed for Carnival processions which consisted of decorated floats and plenty of fancy dress costumes. Some towns, like Loulé, were famous for their parades, with scantily-clad Brazilian dancers braving the Algarve winter and politically satirical floats. In Carvoeiro, it was usually led by the local biker club racing around the village, followed by the procession on both the Sunday before, and on the day itself. A wave of fun rolled out, brightening up the end of winter. Spring, as usual, arrived early in the Algarve and the first buds appeared on the almond trees in mid-January.

Legend had it that when the Moors ruled the area, known then as Al-Garb, a prince named Ibn-Almundim fell in love and married a Scandinavian princess called Gilda. They lived in Silves, then the capital of Al-Garb. However, she began to pine for the winter snow in her homeland, so he arranged for thousands of almond trees to be planted around the castle and beyond, so their blossom would look like snow and help her to forget her homesickness. It worked and they lived happily ever after.

This also explained the popularity of almonds amongst the locals. Almonds in the liqueur, Amarguinha, in the marzipan *doces finos*, shaped into fruits, vegetables and animals and the many almond cakes and tarts sold in every cafe and *pastelaria*. It's no surprise that the Portuguese are renowned for having a very sweet tooth.

We managed to bypass the fancy dress section and concentrated on stocking up for our return to the villa that afternoon. They had completed the work and Nick double-checked to find that we did indeed have hot and cold running water again. We tidied the apartment, although the maid would come in and remove all evidence of our presence. Even though we'd tried to keep the sofas covered, I didn't envy her the task of cleaning up all the dog hairs we left behind. Our next clients weren't booked in until Easter, so she had plenty of time. The villa had also been cleaned and it was a relief to be back, plus the cats were pleased to see us too.

Over the next few weeks, we fell back into a routine. Nick stayed busy, he had a good reputation and lots of recommendations. He also started doing deliveries for a local furniture shop and made a lot of contacts that way too. I did my 3 days a week in the office, popping home in my 2-hour lunch break to let the dogs out and relax on the terrace. I also found it handy because I could do a few chores like hanging washing out, once Maria had finished for the day.

A small, enclosed courtyard off the kitchen, housed the washing line. The walls stood about 6 feet high and appeared solidly built, with just a wrought iron gate for access, which we usually kept locked. One day, as I happily pegged the clothes out in the sunshine, Samson at my side, a sudden gust of wind blew the kitchen door shut. I turned the handle but the door remained tightly closed, it seemed the bang had dislodged the lock mechanism and of course, I had left the key on the inside, as well as my bag and phone and knew there were no neighbours close enough to hear me shout for help.

Samson and I were locked in a space about 4 feet x 6 feet with no water, no shade and no way out. I could never climb the smooth walls and anyway, there was a 6-foot drop on the other side. Even if I could get out, I couldn't get back in the house and Nick wasn't due back for hours. I stood there, completely stuck and out of ideas when I heard footsteps on the gravel and someone whistling as they approached the house. In my panic, I had forgotten it was Wednesday, Fernando's gardening day.

"Senor Fernando?" I shouted.

"Estou sim?"

How could I even describe my predicament? In very garbled Portuguese, I made a stab at it.

"Muito vento, porta fechada!" I shouted.

Silence.

Then a scraping sound and first his cap and then his face appeared, looking down at me over the wall. He took off his cap and scratched his head. I went over to the door and showed how it was stuck fast. He leaned further over, checking the courtyard for inspiration, obviously, none came and he disappeared again. I checked my watch and realised that I should have been back at work 15 minutes ago. I'd only been there a few weeks and this wouldn't look good. Edward probably thought I'd gone for an afternoon nap and even if he had tried to call me, he wouldn't have received any reply.

Fernando appeared again.

"Janelas - abertas?"

What windows? Oh, did he mean the patio doors?

"São abertas, sim," I replied, remembering that in Portuguese you rarely reply to a question with a simple yes or no but repeat the verb, adding *sim* or *não* if required. Anything else sounded a bit abrupt and unfriendly to the Portuguese ear.

He disappeared and I heard the dragging sound again; he must have brought his ladders up from the garden. I heard him go past the other side of the courtyard which led to the steps between the house and the pool. Roughly halfway down the steps brought one level with the front balcony. If he could scramble across the shrubbery, he might just be able to climb over the wall. I could hear muttering, and scraping and exclamations and then silence - then footsteps coming from inside the house. I could hear the door handle rattling and after a few attempts, the door burst open. Oh, Fernando, I could have kissed him. His hands were scratched and there was a hole in his trousers that I couldn't be 100% certain had just happened but he'd rescued us. I wasn't quite sure how to express my gratitude but as I tried, he just looked a bit embarrassed and waved a hand.

"Não há problema."

I opened the fridge and grabbed some bottles of beer. He accepted only two and raised them in a 'cheers' motion.

"Saúde!"

"Saúde," I replied, "e muito obrigada."

He nodded in acknowledgement and went back to his work as if this was an everyday occurrence. I grabbed my things and locked up, hurrying back to the office and hoping that Edward would believe my excuse for my unexpected absence.

Fernando had really gone out of his way to help me, something we had experienced time and time again since moving here. It would recur a few years later when I found myself facing major spinal surgery.

10

February 2008 - Doctors

As I went to stand up from my desk one February morning, I discovered I couldn't. My back had suddenly 'gone'.

I had been diagnosed with scoliosis, curvature of the spine, at the age of 10 or 11, following a fall on a school skiing trip. Many appointments with specialists in London later, the consensus at that time said best to leave it alone, surgery deemed too risky. Consequently, I lived with constant back pain and restricted movement for years. It became normal that I couldn't sit in a chair for long and car, train and plane journeys proved a nightmare but I almost forgot the reason for it. I had also consulted an orthopaedic consultant about 10 years before when he took one look at my current x-ray and commented:

"Of course, it's going to hurt, look at the state of it," and promptly left the room, so that was that.

This time, I couldn't ignore it; I was in terrible pain and unable to walk. So, I embarked on the path that would eventually lead to major spinal surgery in a Lisbon hospital. A difficult, painful, frustrating time followed but not without its lighter moments, which, at times, managed to take my mind off the situation.

After several months of trying different medications and physiotherapy, I knew my back hadn't improved, it was actually getting worse. My physiotherapist, Alison, realised there had been a major deterioration in my spine and as well as scoliosis,

I was also suffering from spondylolisthesis. This meant that the vertebrae had become unstable and were sliding away from each other, endangering my spinal cord and risking paralysis. She suggested I saw a neurosurgeon to get his opinion and I made an appointment at a hospital in Faro. Alison kindly offered to accompany us, so we all arrived, complete with MRI scans, to find a double of Theo Paphitis, who took one look at my spine and said:

"Wow, this needs surgery!"

Not only had the curvature got worse, but my spine was also now unstable and according to Theo:

"If I don't operate, one day your spine will break," which he demonstrated with a twig-snapping gesture.

I knew I had no choice, the operation had to go ahead to straighten and fuse my spine. We booked a private appointment, thinking I might need a small operation and expected to pay 5-8.000€. However, Theo was very direct.

"I hope you have insurance?"

"Yes, I do have insurance but as the scoliosis is a pre-existing condition, it isn't covered."

"This is going to be very expensive," he replied. "At least 25.000€, but it could be much more, depending on what I find when I open you up," he grinned wolfishly. "Whether there are complications, how long you need to stay in intensive care."

Not only was I shocked to hear that I needed such major surgery but the figures he kept quoting just seemed ridiculous. I know you are supposed to think that health is more important than money but how could I spend that much on my back? To top it all, the operation would have to be done in a Lisbon hospital as those in the Algarve could never deal with such complicated surgery.

Fortunately, we worked here legally and paid tax and social security contributions, so Theo suggested I have the operation done on the Portuguese state health system. He would make sure that I was put on his waiting list, which at the time was not too long, so off we went up to Lisbon, to register as a patient at the hospital.

We had spent a long weekend in Lisbon in 2007, so we knew our way around and luckily the hospital was in a fairly central location. We booked the train tickets to travel up the day before and spent the night in a nearby hotel. We found the Portuguese train service from the Algarve to Lisbon excellent and extremely good value, at around 25€ per person each way, for a first-class, reserved seat and the trains ran on time; easily the best way to get to and from Lisbon.

My appointment was for 9 am, so we arrived at the out-patients department by taxi at 8.45 am. Eventually, I found the person Theo had told me to contact; I filled in the various forms required and they directed me to a nearby waiting area. As usual, we had to take a ticket at the 'senha' machine near the entrance and find a space to await the great man's arrival. We found the only place free in the already crowded waiting area, next to an old, unused senha machine.

A few minutes later, a newly-arrived patient walked up to the machine and started pressing the buttons randomly, with increasing irritation. I leant over and explained that the machine was out of order and pointed to the nice, shiny, new machine that she had just walked past as she came in. She turned around, muttering and went off to get her ticket. As soon as she left, another patient hopeful of obtaining a senha appeared. I repeated the directions to the functioning machine, then came another and another. As we waited for Theo to arrive, giving out directions to the correct machine became almost a full-time occupation. I could only assume a recent change had occurred and everyone was used to getting their senhas from this machine.

Across the corridor from our seats, I noticed a public toilet which also appeared to be out of order; no sign on the door, but it seemed to be locked and we never saw anyone emerge. A pattern quickly established where the unsuccessful senha-seeker would turn around and try the handle of the toilet door, assume it was engaged and stand waiting for it to become vacant. So, after intervening regarding the senha machine, I would then pop up again, explaining that the toilet was unoccupied and presumably not working. I'm sure the Portuguese patients must all have wondered how a foreigner had become so well-acquainted with their hospital.

We waited and waited and as my back made it very uncomfortable to sit, I stood upright, shifting from foot to foot, trying to take the pressure off my spine. I must have looked in a bad way because a tiny, elderly, Portuguese lady, well into her eighties and so small, you felt you could pick her up and put her in your pocket, offered me her seat. I had to refuse her kind offer.

We were the only foreigners there, probably the only 'estrangeiros' in the whole hospital, surrounded by Portuguese, who accepted a lengthy wait for any kind of officialdom as normal. As we continued to wait, another elderly lady came up to us and started a conversation. Again, perfectly normal in the circumstances, as the Portuguese love to talk and will happily while away the hours waiting for their number to be called, chatting away to anyone and everyone. However, this lady was asking for our help. I'm not quite sure why she chose us, the 'estrangeiros', but she grabbed hold of my arm and dragged me over to the vending machine in the corner, wanting to know how to use it. I asked her what she wanted, and she pointed to a small cake, costing 80 cents.

She opened her purse but showed me that it didn't contain any change, so I put a 1€ coin into the machine and showed her how to press the buttons for the numbers corresponding to the desired cake. I removed it from the machine and handed it to her and she thanked me and sat down to eat it. Nick looked across, raised his eyebrows and shrugged but I had done my good deed for the day.

Time dragged on, we still hadn't seen any sign of Theo and none of the other patients seemed to be waiting to see him. I was beginning to wonder if we were in the right place. We were discussing going back to the reception area to check when I felt a tap on my shoulder. I turned around to see an elderly Portuguese man pointing at the vending machine; not again! I was beginning to wonder if we had been set up for some sort of Candid Camera programme. Then I heard: "Muito Obrigado," and saw the cake woman waving across the room at me, her husband had come to say thanks and gratefully shook hands with both of us. After several minutes of smiling and nodding and obrigados, he went back to his wife and just as they turned towards the exit, Nick murmured:

"And he still didn't pay you for the cake!"

The waiting room grew more and more crowded. Now and

again the loudspeaker crackled into life announcing a patient's name and the room number for their consultation and everyone turned expectantly to see which lucky person was being called. I found it hard to make out the names, but as long as someone got up and went towards the right room, I knew it wasn't my turn.

At about 11.15, a white coat whisked past. Theo! I was right, no one else was waiting for him, he had come just to see me and officially add me to his waiting list. He didn't even have a consulting room and we wandered around behind him while he looked for an available space. Finally, the three of us squeezed into a tiny, windowless box of a room and he produced the many forms that had to be filled in. As we went through my medical history, he suddenly stopped, delved into his pocket and produced a fruit-flavoured chewy sweet.

"Sorry, I didn't have breakfast," he said and popped it into his mouth, not setting the best example on the health and nutrition front.

Once we had completed and signed the forms, he handed them to me and delivered a rapid-fire set of instructions.

"Take this form to the third floor of the building opposite and give it to the neurosurgery ward secretary. Take this one to the third floor of this building and make an appointment with the anaesthetist. Take this one to your doctor and arrange for all these pre-op tests to be done; bring the results back to the anaesthetist in a few weeks. I plan to do your operation at the end of November."

And that was it. The process had begun. It was really going to happen.

Off we went to find the neurosurgery secretary. Across courtyards, upstairs, along corridors, finally ending up in a very old part of the hospital that looked extremely dark and depressing. My heart sank. The ward was painted in dark brown, peeling paint and I was none too happy at the thought of being admitted here. We handed in the form and set off for the anaesthetic department. Luckily, we only found a short queue as it was now 11.45 and we had to check out of the hotel at noon.

Back home, I made appointments for an ECG, x-rays and blood tests. All turned out fine, so we headed back up to Lisbon for the appointment with the anaesthetist. Back on the train, back to the hotel and a nice surprise when we checked in. Due to a mix up over the taxi we had booked to take us to the station when we left the last time, they had upgraded us to a suite. The next morning, we went back to the hospital at 8.30 for an 8.45 appointment. Another crowded waiting room, another senha machine, thank goodness this one was working perfectly. We handed in all my paperwork and waited, and waited, and waited. The first patient was seen at about 9.30, so we had already been there for an hour and I wasn't even first in. More and more patients arrived, the waiting area filled up, until standing room only prevailed. I found it so painful to sit, I paced up and down, at least it freed up another seat.

The Portuguese tended to stay very patient in these situations. They came prepared, with friends or family - sometimes their whole family - and often started by unpacking a picnic. They happily offered filled rolls and cakes to anyone in the immediate vicinity, striking up conversations and generally getting settled for the duration.

An elderly man in a wheelchair was pushed into the waiting area by someone who I assumed was his grandson. Two other men accompanied them and produced bags of cakes from the local pasteleria along with coffees from the vending machine in the corridor. They flung themselves into a very lively conversation, carried on at high volume in the Portuguese way. We couldn't make out a word they said as they all seemed to lack the optimum number of teeth, but it all sounded very good-humoured.

Suddenly, a female voice piped up from around the corner. I couldn't see the woman at first but she joined in at full volume and whatever she added to the discussion obviously proved highly amusing judging by the smiles appearing around us. A gentle mocking and rivalry appeared to set in, between the relative merits of Lisbon and Porto. The group provided excellent entertainment, the men teasing and the woman pretending to be shocked but giving as good as she got. A few more patients got the call to see the doctor and seats became vacant next to the man in the wheelchair. His adversary took the opportunity to move next to him, although their new proximity did nothing to lower the volume and they continued to talk to each other as though from opposite ends of the corridor.

The conversation sounded increasingly personal. They started asking each other's names and now and again he would say something which would cause her to hold her hands up to her face and let out a short scream in mock horror, whilst he chuckled to himself and his friends as if he had made some improper suggestion. How frustrating not to be able to follow this conversation. The woman rummaged around in her handbag and brought out her purse, unfolding an expanding concertina photo album of sepia and black and white family snaps and proceeded to discuss each one in detail, naming each person, the year they were born, relationship to herself and the previous person and providing a potted family history.

One of the friends then produced a mobile phone and started to take photos and videos of the couple and I got the distinct feeling that we were witnessing the start of a romance. Many of the other people in the waiting area now openly observed them but the couple carried on chatting, totally unconcerned.

Finally, I got the call. The anaesthetist gave me the all-clear and we returned home to wait for the date of the operation, disappointed that we couldn't hang around to see the friendship develop.

They told me to phone the hospital the week before the planned date, to confirm whether the op would go ahead. I made the call as arranged, only to find out that it had been cancelled due to a lack of beds and a provisional date was made for a fortnight later. I felt elated; another two weeks during which I could forget all about it.

Two weeks later, I made the dreaded phone call for a second time; cancelled again. Hooray!! The op now wouldn't take place until after Christmas; I could forget about it all over again.

January came around and I called for the third time.

"Yes, your operation is booked for next Thursday. Please come to the hospital on Wednesday morning."

Bugger.

11

4 Years Earlier, Back at Work

I was enjoying my job and meeting all the various people who came into the office. When it was someone who wanted to sell, we arranged an appointment to view the property, take photos and agree on a sales price. Then after they had signed a contract, we would start to advertise it on a small card in the window and contact a list of prospective buyers who had registered for that type of property. Quite often it concerned a property that Edward had sold before, sometimes even several times, so we could dig out the previous details from the files and update them as necessary.

I found prospective buyers particularly interesting. I liked to spend time chatting to them to find out exactly what they were looking for, then compile a list of places to show them.

After a couple of weeks of finding my feet, Edward took me with him to deal with a new property up for sale. My job was to write down all the main features of the apartment, which would later be fleshed out into a full description and to take some good photos for the cards in the window. It was a small one-bedroom apartment but had been well-maintained with a new kitchen and bathroom, so I duly noted it all down and took several photos. Edward stepped out onto the balcony, overlooking the communal swimming pool.

"This would make a good shot!" he shouted. "The pool looks nice and inviting and you can see the Monchique hills in the background."

"Ok," I called back. "I'll be out in a minute; it's not easy getting a good photo of this bathroom."

As I had thought during my interviews, Edward proved easy to get on with and we had already fallen into a friendly, chatty relationship. I never found him a strict boss and I really appreciated his sense of humour. Both he and Elaine turned out to be great workmates. We took the job seriously, offered our clients a professional service but on our own, we could have a laugh and a lot of good-natured teasing ensued.

I stepped out to join him on the balcony.

"Hm, there's a few clouds coming across now, I think we'll have to change places," I said.

The balcony became fairly narrow at this point, before opening out into a large square, so we had to almost squeeze past each other.

Click.

"What was that?" I asked.

"What?"

"That click."

"I didn't hear anything," he said.

I raised my eyebrows and tried the door handle.

"It's locked."

"Oh," he said, looking shocked. "How did that happen?"

"You must have slid it closed when we changed places."

"I don't think so."

"Not on purpose, but I think you must have caught the handle on your sleeve or pocket."

Edward leant forward to try the door, it was definitely locked. Quite a few patio doors had turned up with this so-called security feature, otherwise known as a design fault, whereby sliding the lock home made them impossible to open from the outside. Well, this apartment was now so secure we couldn't get back in.

We scanned the pool terrace. The weather had turned cool and breezy, so no sun-worshippers lay stretched out on the loungers or braved a dip in the swimming pool. Once again, my bag and phone languished inside the building and Edward never carried a mobile phone. I made a mental note to start strapping my phone to my person. The wind strengthened and it felt really quite chilly standing on the balcony.

"Olà. Ajude-nos!" shouted Edward, several times but with no response.

It was almost lunchtime and I felt quite hungry. I also needed a trip to the loo. A cold wind always has that effect, plus knowing you can't go, means you absolutely must.

We looked around again. Further along the path, we saw a maid leave one of the neighbouring apartment blocks, carrying her bucket of cleaning supplies. We shouted but she turned and walked in the opposite direction.

Edward screamed at the top of his lungs:

"AJUDE-NOS!"

She hesitated and looked around, but not up, and was about

to carry on walking when in desperation, Edward picked up a large beach ball left behind by previous clients and hurled it towards her. It floated along on the breeze for a while, then the colours must have caught her eye because she finally looked up as he belted out another impassioned plea.

"Senhor!" she exclaimed, looking shocked. "Precisa de ajuda?"

Edward nodded until his head almost rolled off and followed the beach ball while waving his arms in the air and beckoning her to come closer. She dropped her bucket and hurried along the path, pulling keys out of her apron pocket.

"Chaves!" she shouted, waving them triumphantly, before disappearing inside the communal entrance door directly below us.

We heard her footsteps approach and the front door opening. When she appeared at the patio door, I had never been so pleased to see anyone before nor since. And I always check patio doors before I step out onto a balcony.

As March arrived, the weather slowly warmed up. When we were at home, we had taken to leaving the kitchen door propped open with a stone, to allow some extra heat and light into the kitchen. One Saturday morning, as we enjoyed a leisurely breakfast on the terrace, we saw Catkin running around the garden. She was being unusually playful, hiding then stalking some fallen leaves which had escaped Fernando's attentions, then jumping and catching them. We watched her for a while, amused at her antics, then headed in to tidy the kitchen and wash up.

Oh, the luxury of a no-Maria day. I was just finishing putting the cutlery away when I caught a movement out of the corner of my eye. Something had walked through the open door and on into the living room. I followed quickly in case it was some kind of wildlife or even a bird. I arrived just in time to see Catkin, tail held proudly aloft, as she stalked into the room. She passed the dogs, stretched out on the sofa, without so much as a glance, jumped onto an armchair and started to give herself a good wash. The dogs didn't move a muscle, I think they were in shock. They had never seen a cat at such close quarters, and one that hadn't shown the slightest fear. They clearly didn't know what to do. I called Nick in from the kitchen.

"Have a look at this!"

"What?"

"Just come here and look, and don't make any noise."

He crept into the living room and stared.

"Is that Catkin? Where did she come from?"

"She just walked in through the kitchen and went past the dogs. I think she's decided to move in."

And indeed, she had, and she stayed, and the dogs accepted her completely.

Anne-Marie and Steve had now decided to rent out their apartment for holiday lets and moved to a place about 10 minutes' drive from Carvoeiro, very much a traditional Algarve village, not a tourist resort, which appealed to them both. They had rented a small, typical whitewashed cottage down a narrow street, while they tested out living a more authentic Portuguese life. The cottage had tiny windows with heavy wooden shutters, set in thick stone walls and designed to stay cool. However, a log burner helped to keep it cosy when the temperature fell. Although small, it had a bedroom, shower room, compact kitchen, sitting area, dining area and a small courtyard.

A keen chef, Steve invited us over for dinner, so he could test out the kitchen facilities. We had a fun evening, enjoying plenty of delicious food and even more delicious wine. When it came time to leave, Anne-Marie and Steve decided to walk with us to our car, which we had left a short distance away, their road being too narrow to park in. We gathered up coats and bags and stepped out in single file through the small front door.

"Don't forget the key!" shouted Anne-Marie to Steve who was bringing up the rear.

We started walking, leaving the boys to lock up and heard Steve slam the door behind him.

"Did you say you've got the key?" he shouted.

"No," shouted Anne-Marie. "I said don't forget the key!"

"Oh, I thought-,"

"What, what did you think?"

"I thought you said I've got the key," he said, joining us.

Anne-Marie sighed and looked at her watch.

"It's gone 11 o'clock, how are we going to get back in now?"

Nick and I hesitated; we knew we needed to get back to let the dogs out but didn't want to leave them stranded.

"Do you want to come back with us?" I suggested. "Then get a locksmith tomorrow?"

Anne-Marie shook her head.

"I've just remembered I haven't blown the candles out," she said.

This added to the rising panic; their cat was also inside and risked setting fire to the place.

"I wonder if Declan will still be up?" said Steve. "He's our landlord, he lives on the other side of the village. We could go and see if there's a light on?"

"Ok, no harm in having a look," said Anne-Marie.

She and I set off in search of a spare key, leaving the boys behind.

"I was sure he heard me," she muttered as we hurried through the deserted streets.

It didn't take long to reach Declan's and we saw a faint sliver of light from beneath the shutters.

"Do you think he's still up?" said Anne-Marie, nervously. "It looks as though there's a light on, but it could be a reflection from the street light."

"Well, there's one way to find out," I replied, helpfully.

"I don't want to disturb him. We've only been there a few weeks; I don't want him to think we'll be knocking every five minutes."

"It's up to you, but if you're going to knock, you'd best do it now, it's only going to get later."

"Ok, I'll just knock quietly; then if he's asleep, he won't hear."

She stepped up and tapped on the door with the tiniest of raps. Nothing happened.

We turned and had just started to walk away when the door opened and there stood Declan, resplendent in striped dressing gown and slippers.

"Oh, sorry, did we wake you?" stuttered Anne-Marie.

"No, not at all, I was just reading before going to bed. Is everything ok? No problems at the cottage?"

"Everything's fine, well, sort of, I mean, we've managed to lock ourselves out and wondered if you had a spare key?"

The words tumbled out while I stood to one side, trying to remain invisible. I hadn't met Declan before and didn't actually meet him this time either. I couldn't bring myself to raise my eyes above ankle level.

"Sure, no problem. I'll just get it."

He turned and disappeared inside the house, quickly returning with the promised key.

"Thanks so much, I'm really sorry to have disturbed you, we'll be more careful I promise," said Anne-Marie, backing away holding the key in her clenched palm, and we rushed back to the cottage.

We found Steve and Nick still standing in front of the doorway but looking slightly shifty.

"We've got the key!" said Anne-Marie, waving it in the air. "Declan was still up and was fine about it."

She stopped short because while she was talking, the boys had stepped apart, revealing an open door.

"How did you manage that? Did you have the key after all? We walked all the way to Declan's and disturbed him!"

"No, no key," laughed Nick. "Just this," and held up his supermarket loyalty card. "It opened the lock in seconds."

12

Moving house

We had rented the villa for six months, which, unbelievably, was coming to an end. We had approximately a month to find somewhere else to live before the Easter holiday-makers arrived. Now I was working in the village, we would really have to stay nearby but availability diminished in summer and the prices rose alarmingly. Instead of 1000€ a month, our current villa would increase to more than 1000€ a week in July and August. We went back to scouring the local newspapers and the village online forum for possibilities. I saw one place and almost immediately discounted it as it had just one bedroom, but Anne-Marie and Steve just had one bedroom in the cottage in Pêra.

"Do you think we could manage in a one bed?" I asked Nick. "There's a small house for rent for 500€ a month plus bills but it's got quite a big enclosed garden and fantastic sea views."

He thought for a moment.

"I suppose it's worth a look, there's not much else around just now."

We rang the contact number and arranged to view it the following day.

We had a rough idea where it was, above the cliffs at Algar Seco but had some trouble finding the exact house. We came across three or four rows, each containing a terrace of four small houses. There was also a distinct lack of numbers and those that were numbered didn't seem to follow any pattern. We had to resort to ringing the agent to give us more precise directions.

Of course, it turned out to be the first row we had come across; we just hadn't driven far enough down the narrow track. The house stood second from last, at the end of a cul-de-sac.

The first good point I noted, it had a driveway, otherwise, we'd have to park a mile away. We pulled in behind the agent's car and made our way down the drive, passing a washing machine sitting under an awning to our left, opposite the front door to our right. The door stood open, so we gave it a quick tap and shouted:

"Hello!" as we walked straight into the living room.

We found the agent in the middle of the room with his back to us, but as he turned to face us, we suddenly realised what he'd been staring at, the most incredible, breath-taking view we could ever have dreamed of. The sea stretched forth from the end of the garden and we could hear the waves crashing against the cliffs.

"Pretty amazing, isn't it?" he said as he came over to shake hands. "I'm Pieter, pleased to meet you."

"Yes, it's fantastic, imagine waking up to that every morning?" said Nick.

I could tell he was sold, even before we had looked around the place.

"So, this is the living room, as you can see," Pieter smiled and gave a slight shrug. "There is the kitchen, there is the bathroom and there is the bedroom."

We could see into all the rooms from where we were

standing. Compared to the rambling villa it felt like being in a doll's house. We'd never lose each other here.

Pieter took a step towards the French doors.

"Here is a small balcony and down the steps is the garden."

We followed him onto the balcony and looked down on 50 square feet of grass and shrubs, surrounded by 6 feet high walls, perfect for the dogs. It also had the obligatory internet already installed.

"We'll take it, when can we move in?" we almost said in unison.

We paid a deposit there and then, relieved to have somewhere to move to. The house became available in two weeks, giving us a fortnight's overlap and plenty of time to prepare for the move. Although the house was tiny, I so looked forward to living there. Also, situated closer to the village, it gave me an easier walk to work and I couldn't wait to have that wonderful view every day.

For my first few viewings with prospective clients, either Edward or Elaine had accompanied me, but gradually I was allowed to go out on my own. The first time I picked up those keys, I felt extremely nervous. The clients had agreed to meet me at the villa, so I left plenty of time to open the place up to show it at its best.

It was a modern, 5-bedroom villa with en-suite bathrooms, a large pool and terrace, aircon, outside kitchen and barbecue area and electric shutters. These were kept closed, partly for security reasons but also to keep the interior cool and to prevent the soft furnishings from fading in the strong sunlight. It was located on a small development, along the coast road towards the next village. As I drove there on that bright sunny morning, I realised just how lucky I was. The road ran parallel with the sea, sparkling blue in the sunshine, no traffic in either direction and I was making my way to a beautiful villa. This was my life now and they even paid me to do it. Wow!

I pulled into the stylish, tiled driveway and found the key for the heavy front door. Inside, everything felt silent and still, immaculately furnished, just waiting for someone to fall in love with it. I rushed around opening all the electric shutters: one in each bedroom; two in the living room; one in the dining room. The sun streamed in and I just had time to unlock the patio doors to the pool area and compose myself, before I heard a car pull up and voices of people approaching the front door.

The viewing passed really well and the clients left, promising to have a chat over lunch and call into the office in the afternoon. I had a good feeling about this; maybe I'd get my first commission. I went around closing all the shutters, double-checking that I'd locked the door to the pool, then the front door and set off back to the office.

When I arrived back at the office, I found Edward and Elaine keen to know how my first solo viewing had gone.

"It was great," I said. "I think they might be interested. They said they'll call in later and let us know."

"That sounds promising," said Edward. "And how is the house looking, all in good order?"

"Yes, it's immaculate, but it's hard work going round and opening up all the shutters, isn't it?" I replied as I hung my coat on the back of my chair.

The two of them burst out laughing,

"What's so funny? Am I not supposed to open the house up?"

Edward was helpless, leaving Elaine to carry on.

"Did you go into every room, what, three times?" she asked.

"Yes, once to open, once to close and once with the clients."

"Did you not notice the control panel by the front door?"

"No, what control panel?"

Edward by now had almost slid off his chair, but seeing my face, he pulled himself upright.

"I'm sorry, I thought I told you," he said, trying to look contrite. "The panel by the front door controls all the shutters, you can open and close them from there, individually... or, together." A tiny smile sneaked across his lips.

"You mean I spent all that time getting flustered, in and out of all those rooms?"

"I'm really sorry, I really thought I had told you," Edward was now hiccupping in an attempt to keep a straight face.

"I won't forget this, you know," I warned, but I was laughing now too. "Just watch out!"

We met Pieter again to pick up the keys to the Algar Seco house. He showed us where the gas bottles were stored and the electricity meter, so we could keep an eye on the readings and how much we were using. On closer inspection, the kitchen was minute, with space for only one person at a time and apart from a few cupboards, it offered just a sink, hob and oven.

"Is there a washing machine?" I asked.

Pieter laughed and carried on showing us a cupboard containing some spare bulbs and batteries. I looked at Nick and gestured towards Pieter, maybe he'd have more luck.

"Erm, yes, we were wondering if there was a washing machine?" he repeated.

Pieter looked up.

"Oh, yes, sorry, I thought it was an English joke. I know you have a good sense of humour."

"No," I stressed. "We really were asking about a washing machine."

"You just walked past it," said Pieter, pointing towards the front door. "There it is."

The three of us were now staring at the washing machine, which of course we had just walked past.

"Does it work? I mean, is it plumbed in and plugged into the electrics?" I asked, having assumed it was an old one waiting to be dumped.

"Yes, it works, of course." He lifted a corner of the awning and exposed the plumbing and wiring. 'It's all perfectly fine, protected from the rain, and the sun."

`It didn't look very protected to me, but I guessed we'd just have to take his word for it. At least we would only be here until about September so there shouldn't be too much rain to worry about.

Nick's van came in handy as we packed our few belongings, plus some boxes that we hadn't bothered opening so far. On my days off and at the weekend, we slowly moved across to the other side of the village. There remained only one precious item, that we weren't sure if we should move, Catkin. We knew she had come from the villa next door and that the owners were paying someone to come and feed the cats every day; we had bumped into him several times. But Catkin was really part of the family now, along with Ginger and Camões and we wanted to take all three with us. The kittens we knew were strays but I wasn't sure about Catkin.

During our final week in the villa, we noticed a car had appeared in the drive next door, a German registered 4x4 and we guessed it belonged to the owners. Every time we walked past, we glanced across until one evening we saw two figures on the balcony, watching the sunset. They waved at us and Nick waved back, then stood for a while trying to make it obvious that he wanted to chat. The man stood up and came over to the side nearest us.

"Good evening," he said.

"Good evening," Nick replied. "We're from next door, we have been renting there for the winter."

"Ja, I know, my friend who feeds the cats, he tells me."

"Well, it's about the cats- well, one of the cats we wanted to talk to you about."

"Ja? Problem?"

"No, well I hope not."

"Please, come in and tell me."

We opened the gate and went up the steps to greet them. They introduced themselves as Gerhard and Inga and proved extremely hospitable.

"Sit, please, we are just enjoying a glass of wine. Would you like to join us, or maybe a beer?"

We accepted the drinks and took our seats; then tried to explain about Catkin. They looked confused.

"She's a small cat, a lot of white but with some grey tabby patches and bright blue eyes," I said.

"Ah, that is Lucy," Gerhard smiled. "She is one of my favourites; I always look for her when we come. I wondered where she was."

"Actually, she's with us. She decided to come into the house one day and now she stays in almost all the time."

I hoped he would understand that we hadn't stolen her but that she had moved in of her own free will.

"Ah, that is a little sad for me but I think it is very good for Lucy. You know, when we are in Germany I worry a lot about her, but if she is happy with you, I don't need to worry more."

"Yes, she seems very happy with us, but we have to leave next week…" Nick trailed off and Gerhard's smile disappeared.

"Oh, and Lucy?"

"Erm, well she can come too. We will still be in the village, but I don't want to take her away from you?"

Gerhard thought for a moment.

"Of course, she can go with you. I would be very happy to see her in a family. I think it is a perfect solution."

I let out a sigh of relief, I thought for a minute it was going to be awkward but Gerhard did just want the best for her, thank goodness. They poured more drinks to toast Lucy, then brought us her vaccination card and cat box and a carrier bag full of food.

We left as friends that night and Lucy became officially ours; we could take her with a clear conscience and with their blessing. Lucy lived with us until she was 17 and Gerhard and Inga visited every time they came over, each time bearing a big bag of food and treats.

13

January 2009, Lisbon – Hospital

The next few days were a whirlwind of organisation, with train tickets and a hotel room to book, as Nick would stay in Lisbon for at least the first few days. The animals had to be taken into kennels/cattery, bags packed, friends and family notified, then suddenly Tuesday came around and off we went.

We arrived at Entrecampos station in Lisbon and walked across the road to the taxi rank. Several cars always stood waiting for fares, so we got into the first one in the queue and asked him to take us to our hotel. The driver, José, spoke quite good English, and chatted away happily, assuming we were tourists on holiday – if only. I explained that we lived in the Algarve and that I was going into hospital for an operation on my spine; so we switched to Portuguese while he explained that he knew the hospital as his wife had been operated on there, twice, very successfully.

As he dropped us off at the hotel, he gave Nick his card and said he would be happy to help in any way he could. He also gave some very useful advice, pointing out where Nick could get the tram to the hospital and how much it would cost. I felt a bit preoccupied with the thought of the operation, but I appreciated his kindness and concern and he wished me well as Nick paid and waved him off.

The next morning, we set off for the hospital. I felt much calmer than I had expected, but couldn't help being slightly apprehensive of what lay in store. Back up to the dark, depressing neurosurgery ward, we found no one and just waited at the empty office. The secretary we had seen on our previous visit arrived. I gave my name and explained that Theo was due to operate on me the following day. She looked me up on the computer.

"Sorry, you are not being operated on here."

What did she mean I wasn't being operated on here? I had phoned a few days ago and confirmed it. She came out into the corridor and pointed us back the way we had come.

"You are going to be in neuro trauma, not neurosurgery; go through the door, along the corridor and through the next door; they will see to you."

We followed her directions and thankfully came to a much brighter, more modern ward where, once again, I explained who I was, this time to a young nurse, who looked perplexed.

"I don't know if we have a bed for you," she said.

Surely, we hadn't made all these arrangements and a trip up to Lisbon for nothing? She led us into a lounge area, with a TV showing the Portuguese equivalent of Phil and Holly on This Morning and motioned for us to sit and wait. I explained that sitting was very uncomfortable, so she brought in a trolley and said I could lie on it while I waited. It felt a bit strange, but it was the most comfortable place to be so I got up onto the trolley, with some difficulty, and although I was fully clothed, she covered me with a blanket.

Once again, we waited and waited. Theo turned up and said he thought they would have a bed for me after lunch. Various nursing staff came and went, probably wondering what was wrong with the apparently healthy person lying on the trolley. Several elderly patients were brought into the lounge in their wheelchairs and mostly slept through the TV programme. It showed a strange mix of the normal topics of cooking, fashion etc, interspersed with live music when the presenters and audience would get up and dance around the studio. The most frequent performer, an eccentric-looking character with a huge handlebar moustache and wearing a leather trilby, played the programme's theme tune on his accordion. The first time he appeared I assumed we had come to the end of the programme, as the music faded and the adverts followed, but no, 2 or 3 minutes later on it came again. This happened over and over again; the programme lasted for hours, the elderly patients continued to snore quietly, meanwhile, we waited and waited.

Suddenly a porter arrived, checked my name, and started manoeuvring my trolley into the corridor. I asked him where we were going and he replied that he was taking me for pre-op tests.

"But I've already had those done!" I protested, waving my envelope full of test results at him, so he called a nurse over to show her.

"Sorry," she said. "Theo wants you to have them done again."

So that had all been a complete waste of time and off we went to the ECG department.

"Sorry, no one here to do the test at the moment."

He about-turned and whisked me off to x-ray, where I offered to get down from the trolley and stand in front of the machine, as I had done previously at the clinic in the Algarve.

"No, not necessary, we can do it like this," said the

radiographer, one of two men who appeared to perform the x-rays as a Laurel and Hardy tribute act.

"Just take off your bra, but leave your top on," said one of them.

I tried to twist my arms up behind me to undo the clasp but couldn't quite manage it.

"Have you done it yet?" asked the other one.

I shook my head.

"No, sorry."

"Don't worry, we'll help," he said.

They each took up position either side of the trolley and slid one arm around my back, trying to undo the clasp whilst staring straight ahead and fumbling blindly under my top, unsurprisingly without success. I think they were both pushing the strap in the same direction. I'm not sure why they couldn't go behind me and at least look at what they were doing, but perhaps modesty forbade them. Somehow, between the three of us, we managed it and I slid the bra out of my sleeves and placed it on top of the blanket.

Laurel placed the film behind my back and Hardy fiddled with the x-ray machine.

"Breathe in. Wait. That's it. We'll just go and check it's ok."

A few minutes later, they came back.

"Sorry, no good, we'll have to do it again."

I suddenly remembered the back support I was wearing. I didn't know if the supportive strips inside it were made of plastic or metal. Could that be the problem?

"No, your top is too thick."

The top half had pleats, with double the fabric and half a dozen buttons sewn down the middle. Laurel picked up one of the buttons and put it in my mouth. I thought he was joking and started to laugh.

"No, hold the button in your mouth so the pleated area is lifted up and only the single layer of fabric, on the lower part of your top, covers your chest."

I felt sure it would have been much easier all round if I had got off the trolley and changed into a gown, but hey, it was Portugal.

`The porter picked up the x-rays and took me back to the ECG department, along corridors and in lifts, with my bra sitting proudly on top of the blanket. As soon as Nick caught up with us, I passed it to him to hide in a pocket somewhere. Tests completed, we returned to the ward. No sooner had we arrived, than a young nurse came to take a blood sample; from hours of waiting with nothing happening, I was suddenly the centre of attention. It seemed that a bed had been found and I was finally being admitted.

He wheeled me into quite a small room with just two beds, the other already occupied by another woman also being admitted that day. The curtains were drawn around her bed and she sounded very upset. We unpacked my bag and I changed into my nightdress and got into bed as instructed. It seemed a bit strange in the middle of the afternoon but I obeyed orders. The room looked quite spartan, just a bedside locker and a wardrobe per bed. They didn't encourage cards and flowers in Portuguese hospitals, so all you needed was space for spare clothes, toiletries, a bottle of water and maybe a book or magazine. It did however offer a lovely view of the river and the 25th April Bridge. This had been named after the peaceful 'carnation' revolution of 25th April 1974, previously known as the Salazar Bridge after the dictator whose regime they overthrew on that day. And I had the bed nearest the window.

Nick and I chatted quietly whilst various members of staff came in and out, filling in forms, the usual admission process. However, my neighbour just continued sobbing, sounding quite distressed, whilst her husband tried to calm her. I really wasn't looking forward to the long evening ahead.

The curtains around the bed parted and her husband emerged, nodded to us and left the room. Nick stayed a little while longer, I felt reluctant to be left alone with my inconsolable roommate but eventually, it was time for him to make his way back to the hotel. I felt quite strange, lying on the bed thinking about what would happen the following day. I couldn't even concentrate on the book I had brought in, unheard of for me, but I felt oddly calm and not at all anxious, again, not like me at all.

Suddenly the curtains opened again and this time my neighbour appeared, no longer crying. She looked across and smiled at me. We introduced ourselves and it turned out she was East European, not Portuguese, and had been living in Portugal for roughly the same length of time as us. Coincidentally, she also came from the Algarve, where she lived with her husband and two children. She worked in the daytime as a cleaner and in the evenings, in the kitchen of a local restaurant.

Her life was tough, especially as she had been a qualified nurse in her home country, but couldn't afford the time and money necessary to convert her qualifications, to allow her to work in a Portuguese hospital. So, she cleaned, washed up and peeled vegetables whilst her husband worked as a delivery driver, earning only slightly more than the monthly rent on their apartment. She explained that she felt extremely worried about how they would manage financially after her operation to repair a herniated disc. If she was unable to work for several weeks or months, her employers would find someone to replace her, and apart from the monetary implications, she really enjoyed her work in the restaurant. I now understood why she was so upset, but as we chatted, she seemed to cheer up a bit, telling me about her children and how well they had settled in Portugal. I got the impression it was harder for her and her husband to be away from their home country.

Talking to her made me count my blessings. Her husband had to stay with friends in Setúbal as they couldn't afford for him to stay in Lisbon, whilst Nick was just a few minutes away in a nice hotel. Even though I had negotiated a really good deal on the room rate, it was unthinkable for them to spend several hundred euros on a few nights' stay. Although her life in the Algarve was better than it would have been if she had stayed at home, it was a million miles away from the sunshine, plush villas, golf courses and beaches that attracted the tourists. As with many places, scratch the shiny surface and you will find a much uglier reality; it certainly brought it home to me how lucky we were to be here by choice, rather than necessity; others weren't so fortunate.

A metallic, clanking noise in the corridor heralded the arrival of the dinner trolley. It provided a welcome diversion and something different to talk about. They placed my tray on the table by my bed, with a bowl of soup, a bread roll, a main course of salmon, potatoes and vegetables and a piece of fruit for dessert. It didn't look too bad, but looks can be deceiving. I'm not keen on soup as a starter, especially as it is messy to eat when you are unable to sit up and lying almost horizontal. The salmon was dry and overcooked and tasted of nothing, and the potatoes and vegetables had a distinct air of having been boiled in Dettol; even the apple tasted of disinfectant. I didn't feel that hungry anyway.

After they cleared the trays away, a nurse came in to go through pre-op procedures with us.

"Any dentures?"

"No."

"Medication?"

"Already explained."

"Allergies?"

"No."

"Nail polish?"

"Yes!" from both of us.

"No nail polish in the operating theatre. The doctors need to be able to check your circulation during the operation, so it has to come off."

I hadn't thought of that, in fact, I had intended to give my toenails another coat of their usual navy blue but hadn't got around to it. Unable to bend, I would have had to ask Nick to do it for me, that would have given the anaesthetist a bit of a surprise.

Nail polish remover was the last thing that either of us had thought to pack, so the nurse disappeared in search of some, and two of them returned with a large bottle of acetone and balls of cotton wool. Suddenly our hospital room became a strange kind of reverse beauty parlour and for a few minutes, it resembled a girly night in, with all four of us chatting and laughing as the nurses set about removing all traces of varnish. It certainly lightened the atmosphere and took our minds off our respective surgeries for a while.

It was getting late now, our midnight food curfew approached and we were given a final run-through of the plan for the following morning. They would wake us at 6.30 to have a shower, change into our theatre gowns and sexy surgical stockings, then I would be taken to theatre at about 7.30 with my roommate following close behind. As Theo was operating on us both, that seemed a bit strange, but I knew there would be 3 surgeons involved in my operation so assumed he would take a break from me to attend to her.

Still feeling surprisingly calm, I took one last look out of the window at the bridge, busy with cars and trains crossing, even at almost midnight, and at the Statue of Christ the Redeemer on the opposite side of the river. Both bridge and statue looked beautiful, all lit up in the darkness; not many hospital wards offer such a spectacular view.

The lights snapped on at 6.30; the nurses had arrived to deliver our gowns and stockings. We went off to shower and by the time I got back to the room, my bed had been changed and the nurses were keen to get me ready for the off. One of Theo's assistants came to see me, to go over the operation once more. He told me that he thought it would last about 5 hours and I wouldn't need to go to intensive care afterwards. The thought of coming back to the same familiar room in a few hours felt comforting; hopefully, my roommate and I would feel up to a chat later. After dreading having to spend the previous evening in her company, we had actually got on really well. It was less than 24 hours since we met and yet she hugged and kissed me as I was wheeled away to the operating theatre, wishing me luck and hoping to see me later. It's funny how complete strangers can become very close when thrown together in these circumstances.

The hospital was just coming to life. The staff prepared for a shift change and the corridors filled up with trolleys laden with clean linen, medicines and medical supplies. The night staff yawned as they headed for home. The newly- arrived day staff looked bright and chirpy, calling to each other and greeting the patients as they moved through the ward. It was surreal, the day I had dreaded for months had arrived, but I still felt strangely calm as we arrived in the pre-op area. I was lifted from my bed onto a narrow trolley and pushed into a corridor to wait my turn.

The staff were lovely, almost all who passed by stopped to introduce themselves and check I was ok. The atmosphere stayed very light-hearted, just another day at work to them. I could hear conversations about last night's TV, the weather, their families. The normal chit-chat between colleagues in any shop, factory or office anywhere, however, in this case, they were preparing to operate on my spine.

A young nurse introduced herself and started chatting away. She explained that she had been nursing for 5 years but had transferred to theatre work only a few months ago and was shadowing a more experienced nurse during my operation. I asked her if she had attended an operation like mine before.

"No, not yet," she replied. "I'm really looking forward to it; we don't get the opportunity to see many like yours."

The anaesthetist arrived, coincidentally the same one who had given me the all-clear back in November. She recognised me and joined in the conversation with the nurses, whilst placing various rubber masks over my face, trying them out for size. I was now in the operating theatre, under the lights, suddenly aware that I was still fully awake. They didn't appear to believe in pre-meds in Portugal. I could see the theatre staff getting organised around me, arranging instruments, going through what was obviously a well-planned and rehearsed procedure. The atmosphere stayed calm and casual, with no panic or fuss; no sign of Theo though. I assumed he probably made a grand entrance once his minions had prepared everything for his arrival, it wouldn't do to keep the great man waiting. I looked at the clock, 8.30.

14

2004 – The Little House

We settled into the little house really quickly. It was almost like living in a caravan or holiday chalet, with everything so close to hand; no trailing from one side of the place to the other, no need to shout to find out where Nick was and we never tired of the view. I marvelled at how much the sea changed in a day. Sometimes you could hardly see the horizon as the sky merged with the ocean, then a few hours later, both sky and sea had dissolved into very different and distinct shades of blue. It always gave us something to see and enjoy; at night, the lights of the fishing boats shone in the darkness; during the day, pleasure cruisers passed by and the pirate ship which carried tourists out from Portimao harbour. Several times we were entertained by a pod of dolphins leaping in and out of the water. I spent hours just gazing out to sea.

Back in the office, I had another solo viewing. Nigel and Jenny knew the Algarve well and wanted to sell their current apartment and buy a detached villa. They had asked to see a lovely 3-bedroom property, tucked away down a quiet lane. It had a large garden to the front and rear and was very private. I had high hopes for this viewing and quite a soft spot for the villa.

We met at the house and after showing them around I left them to have another look on their own, while I attempted a conversation with the German owners, not terribly successfully. Thankfully, Nigel and Jenny reappeared fairly quickly and seemed impressed with the house; my hopes of a sale rose higher.

We had a quick chat outside, covering the pros and cons of the villa then they went off to discuss it between themselves. A few days later, they popped into the office and confirmed they would like to make an offer. In the meantime, they had found a buyer for the apartment through a friend, so they were keen to secure the villa. The German owners took a little time considering the offer but eventually accepted it. I had made my first sale. I was really pleased, not just for the commission, but I liked both the house and Nigel and Jenny. We seemed to be on the same wavelength with a similar sense of humour and they were also animal lovers, with a beautiful rescued greyhound.

They had arranged to complete the sale of the apartment, then go back to the UK for the summer and move into the villa when they returned in September. The apartment had a basement that had been used for storage and they started to pack it up ready for the move. A few days later, Jenny called into the office. She looked a bit nervous and I hoped nothing had gone wrong with their sale or purchase.

"Hi, I wonder if you can help us or give us some advice?" she began.

"Yes, if I can, certainly."

"Well, we've started clearing the basement and I think a little kitten is living down there. We haven't seen it very clearly but as we moved some sun loungers, it darted out and hid behind some boxes."

"Oh, how old do you think it is?"

"Pretty young. I thought of you because of the experience you told us about, with Lucy and the kittens. We'll have to catch it and maybe try to re-home it; I hate to think of it down there, especially once we go."

I remembered our conversation about animal rescue, their greyhound and our cats. I'm always a soft touch for an animal in need but I wasn't that experienced at catching feral kittens. We hadn't done such a good job with Camões.

"Well, I'll try, but I don't know if I'll be much help."

"It would be great to have another pair of eyes and hands. We'll empty the basement of anything we can get rid of, then it will have fewer places to hide. Can I give you a ring, maybe next week?"

I agreed and gave her my mobile number, not sure what I was letting myself in for.

Edward always showed a great interest in people; everyone found him easy to talk to and he genuinely enjoyed finding things out. He was curious about the fact that Nick and I, my parents, my sister and her partner had all moved over within a few months of each other. I suppose it seemed a bit strange but we hadn't thought so at the time. We just happened to have found our lives at crossroads for one reason or another and it turned into a fairly logical next step. Edward found it particularly interesting that both Anne-Marie and Steve had both left quite high-profile jobs, mixing with people he considered household names. He brought up the subject during a quiet moment in the office.

"Tell me, what made your sister leave her job? I mean, it must have been very interesting and meeting all those people!"

"I don't really know," I replied. "She'd done it for a long time and maybe just had enough of the pressure."

"Oh, really," he said and gazed into space as if imagining himself in that world. "But it must have been amazing."

"Yes, I think it was," I blithely agreed, mid-way through typing up some property details. "But things aren't always the way they look from the outside."

"No, I suppose not," he murmured then suddenly leant towards me. "Does she look like you?"

"A bit, I suppose. We have different colour eyes, but apart from that we're similar."

The phone rang and he answered it straight away as usual, so that ended the conversation for now.

The following Monday, he burst into the office in his usual energetic manner.

"You know you said your sister had moved to Pêra?"

"Yes, that's right, a couple of weeks ago."

"Well, do you know, we went to the Italian restaurant in Pêra on Saturday evening?"

"Oh, did you? And did you enjoy it?"

"Well, we sat at a table in the corner and could see everyone else in the restaurant; it was very busy."

"That's good," I murmured.

I already knew what was coming but let him continue his story. He was leading up to a big reveal and I didn't want to steal his thunder.

"And do you know, I saw a couple a few tables away and I was sure it must be your sister."

"Really?"

"Yes, I was so convinced, do you know what I did?"

I leaned back in my chair.

"What did you do?"

"I went over and said: 'Excuse me, but are you Anna-Marie?"

"Anne-Marie," I corrected him.

"Yes, Anna-Marie, and do you know, it was!" he finished with a flourish.

131

"Yes," I smiled. "She sent me a text on Saturday evening to tell me."

"Oh, of course," he looked a little deflated. "But don't you think that's amazing? I've never met her before but I just knew she was your sister!"

"Yes, I suppose so. I didn't think we were that alike."

"My dear, you could be twins! And we had a lovely chat and Steve was very nice too. I asked her all about her job."

"Did you? Was it as interesting as you expected?"

"Absolutely. And I was just wondering, what would you think, I mean, do you think she'd be interested in working here?"

"Do we need someone else?"

"Erm, well I wasn't specifically looking for someone else, but maybe she could come in on your days off, a sort of job share?"

"I don't know; you'd need to ask her."

"Good idea, have you got her telephone number?"

Edward obviously felt that Anne-Marie's contacts would be an asset to the office, although I didn't imagine they'd be interested in property in Carvoeiro, but I gave him her number anyway, then texted her to expect a call. She did actually have a job already at The Resident, a local English newspaper, but it was also part-time, so she agreed to job-share with me and for the first time in our working lives, we became colleagues.

The following weekend we all went out for lunch to celebrate our move to our little house and Anne-Marie's new job. The six of us decided to go to a beach bar set up on the cliffs overlooking a nearby beach, one of the biggest in the area and very popular in summer. However, in early April, not even the Easter tourists had arrived yet.

We sat at a table on the terrace and ordered some drinks, while we looked at the menus and caught up on each other's news. As the waitress approached to take our food order, we noticed some dark clouds rolling in from the sea. Even though the weather had started to perk up in March, we'd heard that often a 'false summer' appeared with a few warm sunny weeks. Just as I decided to bring out my summer clothes and pack away the winter ones, Mother Nature reminded us who was really in charge and give us a last taste of winter. This seemed to be turning into one of those days, as a chilly gust of wind blew the napkins off the table and we made the decision to move to a table inside. Within a few minutes, the sky turned completely dark, the wind strengthened and the rain came down. We found ourselves the only customers in the restaurant but at least we were dry and warm.

Our food arrived promptly and we started eating. Outside the weather grew steadily worse. The awning flapped so violently it looked ready to fly off and we witnessed plastic tables and chairs tossed around like toys on the terrace. Huge gusts of wind brought the rain crashing against the floor-to-ceiling windows, which rattled with each blow.

We noticed the staff pushing tables together at the other side of the restaurant, eventually enough to seat about a dozen people. Surely no one would venture out in this storm? The waiters continued to set out plates and cutlery, then baskets of bread and butter, local cheese and the marinated carrots and olives that are part of the 'cover' in almost every Portuguese restaurant.

We had now finished our plates of chicken Piri-Piri, pork and clams and cataplana, a traditional fish stew served in a large curved metal dish, with a matching hinged lid, but there was no way we could leave. I doubted whether we would even be able to open the door. There was only one thing for it:

"Excuse me, could we have another bottle of wine, one bottle of water and three beers?"

Our waitress nodded and brought the drinks over. I couldn't help trying to satisfy our curiosity.

"Are you expecting a big group for lunch?"

She smiled and gestured to the storm rampaging around us.

"No, I don't think anyone will come today."

"Yes, the storm is very bad isn't it. I just wondered about that table over there?"

Another smile.

"That is for us, as we have plenty of food but no clients, the chef is making a big lunch for the staff."

One by one the waiting staff, followed by the kitchen staff took their places at the table, chatting animatedly and opening bottles of wine and water. A few minutes later, the chef appeared and placed several large pans and bowls down the centre of the table and a couple of large cataplanas.

The storm continued to rage; we ordered more drinks and the staff enjoyed their lunch. A couple of hours had passed since we had last eaten and we could see some very tempting cakes and desserts on display, so we had a few of those too. Then coffee and a complimentary glass of port, then another, and as the storm finally subsided, we realised we had been sitting there for nearly 5 hours. We agreed it was probably one of the best lunches we'd ever had.

A day or so later, my phone rang just as I pulled up outside the house on my way home from work.

"Hi!" said Jenny. "We're down here in the basement and we've just seen the kitten again; I don't suppose you could pop over?"

"I've just got in from work, but I could be over in about half an hour. I'll just change into something more suitable. I can see Nick's home so he can sort out our little menagerie."

"Great! See you later."

I rushed in and explained to Nick while digging out some old clothes that didn't matter if they got torn, or even blood spilt on them. I knew from Camões how ferocious even a small kitten could be if they didn't want to be caught. I left him taking the dogs for a walk and got back in the car, heading for their apartment just a few minutes away.

It felt really quite hot in the basement and Nigel and Jenny already looked a little flustered. Just a few boxes and deckchairs remained, stacked up against one wall and the couple appeared ready for action with a cat box, which opened at the top and several old towels. They had primed the box with some cat food bait and we all hoped it would feel hungry enough to be tempted in by the aroma.

We stood in silence, barely moving, trying to signal to each other, but there was no sign of the kitten. Nigel decided to slowly move some of the boxes into the middle of the room, to see if we could spot its hiding place.

As soon as he picked up the first box, it darted out and went behind a folded deck chair. I nudged the cat box closer but it continued to ignore the food. By now, all the boxes stood piled up in the middle of the room, just the deckchairs to go.

We knew as soon as we moved them, the kitten would dart out but in which direction? We each took a towel and crouched down. When catching cats and kittens I've now learned that you get one chance, if you fail then you might as well give up. They're wily little things and once spooked you need to come back another day.

Nigel nodded his head; Jenny and I crouched in readiness. He slid the deckchair along the ground and the kitten shot out, straight towards Nigel who threw his towel over it, scooped it up and poked it into the opening at the top of the cat box. We all rushed to hold the door closed while the kitten yelped and scrabbled to get out. We couldn't risk it getting back out now, but we struggled to get the locks in place and all the time it was throwing itself against the door, desperate to escape. Finally, we managed to slide the last lock into place and we all fell back, hot, sweaty and dusty but mightily proud of mission accomplished. We carried the box upstairs and left the kitten to calm down for a few minutes before I drove it home. I called Nick.

"We've got it. I'll be home in about 10 minutes."

"Ok great, where are we going to put it?"

I actually hadn't thought about it. We were so used to all the spare bedrooms at the villa, but now we only had the living room which opened onto the garden and the bathroom. We had to put it somewhere secure.

"It will have to be the bathroom," I replied. "Just hope I

manage to tame it quickly."

Nigel and Jenny were really grateful and I could see it had lifted a huge weight off their shoulders. By the time I got home, Nick had set up a bed and litter tray in the bathroom and we were finally able to see the little scrap that had caused so much trouble. A pretty little brown tabby, still terrified and showing no signs of wanting to leave its sanctuary. We left it in the bathroom, with the door of the box open, closed the window and left it to get acquainted with its temporary accommodation.

A couple of hours later, I crept in, hoping to see it cuddled up in bed, or at least calmer in the box.

"Nick."

"Yes?"

"Can you come in here for a minute?"

"Ok, I'll put the dogs in the garden and shut the door, just in case it makes a run for it."

"I don't think you need to worry."

"Why?"

He stepped into the bathroom and saw I was holding up an empty box. He checked behind the shower curtain and the towel hanging on the wall at the end of the bath. Nada.

"Are you sure the window is shut?"

"Yes, of course, look at it."

It remained firmly shut and locked as we had left it.

"This is ridiculous, it's a kitten, not Houdini; we've not even opened the door, how can it have escaped?"

"I don't know but it's not in here."

The kitten was even more wily than we had thought. We knew it couldn't get out but it had vanished. We had to find it; I couldn't bear to tell Nigel and Jenny that I'd lost the precious kitten on the very first evening.

Feeling particularly foolish, we left out more food and quickly got ready for bed, then shut the door tightly and hoped for a miracle.

The next morning, I woke early and immediately remembered the kitten. I crept out of the bedroom and opened the bathroom door. The smell hit me straight away; the litter tray had been used and the food had gone. I put the light on and looked around again. It was a complete mystery, where on earth could it hide? I checked behind the toilet, under the cistern, the bath panel was secure, with no gaps that it could squeeze through. That just left the sink, fixed on a ceramic pedestal. I knelt down and felt the back of the pedestal, where I found a large opening from the bottom of the basin to about halfway down. As my hand got closer to the bottom, I heard a slight growl. Gotcha. So, we had well and truly been outwitted by a kitten smaller than my hand. I cleaned up the tray, left some more food and went to tell Nick the good news.

We came up with a cunning plan. We would totally ignore it and not try to catch it, but just keep leaving food and water out. We also left a roll of stiff cardboard and some tape, as our plan involved swift action; if we ever went into the bathroom and caught it out of the pedestal, we'd quickly close up the hole. It took a few days but eventually, we went in and found it outside of its hidey-hole. The kitten must have grown a bit and no longer fit inside the pedestal so easily, but we weren't taking any chances and blocked up the gap.

We still didn't know whether it was a boy or girl and had no way of finding out, as it was still completely feral. I decided it looked like a boy and named him Harry. He rejected the nice bed we made for him, preferring to take up residence on the top shelf of a bathroom trolley that we were using to store clean towels. I still have photos of him buried in a towel looking like ET in the bicycle basket. He still growled every time we went into the bathroom but we persevered; we had no choice.

I took to getting in the bath fully clothed, with a good book and spending an hour reading while Harry glowered at me from his towel nest. I totally ignored him, apart from throwing titbits of chicken or tuna in his direction. It took weeks to get his confidence but gradually he edged closer until one day he jumped up on the side of the bath. I still couldn't touch him but felt I had gained his confidence and could start leaving the bathroom door open.

At first, he was terrified of the dogs and none too keen on the other cats, but they totally ignored his little hisses and growls and he soon gave up trying to intimidate them. As he began to mix with the others, we knew we had to get him vaccinated and health checked. This time I picked him up, swaddled in his favourite towel and pushed the whole lot into his carry box. He was most indignant but in no position to object too strongly.

The vet examined him, wearing the obligatory gauntlets and informed us that Harry was in fact a female. She was now around seven or eight weeks old, in good health and received her first vaccination. A process we'd have to repeat three more times over the next six weeks, but we'd worry about that when we got there. At least we knew she was ok and renamed her Tinker Tiger, for her ferocity.

15

Exploring the Algarve
and Goodbye to a Friend

With the stress of the move over, we decided to explore a bit more of the Algarve. The times we'd spent on holiday had only allowed for a limited time, so we never ventured too far. Now we could afford to get out and about and I had read an interesting article about Farol Island, just off the coast of the eastern Algarve. With my parents primed to keep an eye on the animals, we set off to catch the ferry from Olhão. The weather looked slightly overcast and as the previous day had also been quite cloudy, I didn't know whether it would prove the best time to visit the island.

However, I needn't have worried; as we made our way along the Algarve, the skies brightened and by the time we arrived in Olhão, the sun shone down and it felt lovely and warm. No cars were allowed on the island, so we parked close to the market and made our way to the ticket office to buy our return tickets on the ferry, at a grand total of 3.20 euros per person. The boat appeared quite small, seating around 60 people on two decks; and with only one shop on the island, we soon found ourselves surrounded by locals bringing their supplies over from Olhão in supermarket trollies.

The ferry left promptly at 11 am and we set off past the salt flats, that we had seen from the air when we landed at Faro, full of people digging for clams in the sand. First stop Culatra, at the other end of the island, where most of the people got off but we stayed on as the boat continued along the whole length of the island until we reached the pier at Farol. The journey took about 45 minutes in total. We also could have walked 7 Km along the beach from Culatra to Farol.

We made our way down the narrow paths to the beach on the Atlantic side, with no traffic and no roads, just footpaths. Farol impressed us as a really remarkable place. It felt so quiet and peaceful with absolutely no background noise of traffic or civilisation. We sat on the terrace of one of the few bars, enjoying a cool drink and admiring the view of the sand dunes in front of us, then went for a walk to explore the beach, just the other side of the dunes.

The beach looked spectacular; a wide expanse of golden sand stretched before us and a crystal-clear sea. We had it all to ourselves. Most of the houses were holiday homes belonging to north Portuguese. In July and August, they filled the island then left it almost deserted for the rest of the time. A few permanent residents lived there and it had two restaurants, both of which stayed open all year round, joined by a small café in the summertime. We had lunch at one of the restaurants and enjoyed another walk along the beach before catching the ferry back to Olhão at 4 pm. At this time of year, only 3 or 4 ferries operated each day but of course, they ran more frequently in summer. The beautiful island gave us the perfect 'time out' from our normal busy lives; a paradise for bird-watching and fishing, it was definitely worth the trip.

On Easter Saturday, we formed a team with my parents and entered the Car Treasure Hunt, organised by members of the local chat forum. It started in Lagoa and offered two routes, one clockwise and one anti-clockwise, so we didn't have to follow each other. We registered and collected our instructions, as one of the last teams to set off on the clockwise route. First, we headed for Portimão, then turned off towards Monchique. Our first stop came at the natural spring of Caldas de Monchique, where we had to collect a sample of the famous spring water. The next clue lay in Monchique itself, where we searched for a 'chopper', which turned out to be the rescue helicopter stationed there.

From Monchique, we climbed up to Foía, the highest point in the Algarve. The views were spectacular but the temperature felt noticeably lower than near the coast. We then made our way down to the Quinta de São Bento, where a very confused Portuguese woman wondered why they were suddenly so popular. The building, previously the summer residence of the Portuguese royal family, provided the answer to the next question.

Our next stop occurred in a bar in the middle of the countryside, where a young boy stood waiting for us. According to our instructions, we needed to find Wendolin and although he didn't speak any English, he indicated that we should follow him. We had no idea who Wendolin was but we went around the side of the bar and up some steep steps cut into the side of the hill. At the top, we finally found Wendolin – a pig. I have to admit to wondering if it was going to turn out to be the owner of the bar.

We went in and ordered a round of drinks while looking at the general knowledge questions, worth extra points and all related to Portugal and Portuguese history. Fortunately, my parents had recently spent a weekend in Lisbon and were able to provide the answers to quite a few of the questions.

When we left the bar, we must have left our concentration behind too, as we missed quite a few of the following clues. However, we thought we were back on track when looking for the 'orange seller'. We stopped at what we thought was the right place and bought our kilo of oranges. However, the clue asked for the name of the woman selling the oranges and we were served by an elderly man. Undaunted, we got back in the car only to see another orange stall a few hundred metres further on, so we stopped again. This time mum and dad got out, bought a kilo of oranges and asked the woman her name. She looked at us as if we were mad so we gathered we still hadn't found the right place.

Directly across the road stood another fruit stall and the couple kept looking at us expectantly, so we turned the car around and bought yet another kilo of oranges. This time the woman happily told me her name, which was quite unusual; she even spelt it for me. We got back into the car satisfied that we had answered that question correctly at last.

We arrived at the finishing point to hand in our answers, then dropped mum and dad off home to walk their dogs, while we did the same. A meal and prize-giving took place in the evening and we were almost the last to get back, arriving just as they served the soup. After the first course had been cleared away, the prize-giving started. We came precisely nowhere.

During the rest of the meal, we compared answers with the other teams and found that we hadn't done too badly overall but despite 3 visits and 3 kilos of oranges, we still hadn't found the right orange seller. I wondered what those three stallholders thought we were doing, buying 1 kilo of oranges from each of them, keen to know their names and none of them could say they were in on the joke.

The meal continued with a choice of the main course, followed by a selection of desserts, coffee and liqueurs. The food kept coming, waiters continually re-filled our plates and replaced empty wine bottles with full ones. It was unbeatable value and an ideal place for us to end up, to discuss the day. I knew the party continued at a bar in the village, but lightweights that we were, we went straight home to put our feet up. The good news confirmed that the event had raised 500 euros for the orphanage in Albufeira and we had had a lot of fun in the process.

Many restaurants in Portugal, as with this one, provided a set meal, 'Prato de dia' or dish of the day at lunchtime. This made for excellent value and usually consisted of bread, soup, a choice of two or three main courses, dessert, coffee and half a bottle of wine, all for 8-10 euros. They proved very popular with workmen, so whenever we saw a few trucks parked up outside, we knew we'd found a good value place to have lunch.

The next big celebration was 25th April, the anniversary of the 'Carnation Revolution', so-called because of its peaceful nature, with carnations carried in the barrels of the soldiers' guns. It overthrew the Salazar dictatorship, in power since 1932. Now a bank holiday, we found ourselves woken up by the setting of flares at 8 o'clock in the morning.

Nick started preparing for his annual golf trip, which involved flying back to England for the traditional pre-trip dinner, then a ferry to France for a week's golf. It was the first chance for him to catch up with all his mates since we'd left but I knew he felt worried about leaving me on my own.

"I'll be fine," I said confidently, although I felt a little nervous too.

"I've put a new gas bottle on," he said, "and filled the car with petrol. There's plenty of dog and cat food, so you just need to sort out your own food."

"I'll be fine, don't fuss."

He left for the airport, for his Friday afternoon flight and I looked forward to a peaceful week on my own.

We knew before leaving the UK, that Gem was on borrowed time but she still seemed to be enjoying life. However, that weekend she slowed down a lot, then on Sunday evening, she developed a weakness on one side and had trouble walking. She struggled to her feet but almost immediately lay down again. I had a bad feeling about it and spent most of the night lying on the sofa with her next to me on the floor. The next morning, she was no better. I called Edward to let him know and as another animal lover and dog owner, he understood completely.

"Yes, of course, you must get her to the vet immediately. Can you manage? Nick's away, isn't he?"

"I'll be fine, thanks, I'll take her up there now."

I knew he'd come and help if needed, as would my mum and dad but I felt I had to do this on my own.

Our vet didn't run an appointment system, you just went up and waited until your turn came. They had a bench outside and a small shed for shelter if it was raining. I half-carried her into the car, knowing it would probably be for the last time. No point calling Nick, he would already be on the golf course with his phone turned off. I'd speak to him later.

Only one person waited in front of me, holding a cat box on her lap but as soon as she saw Gem, she ushered me in next.

Carlos, the vet, remembered us from operating on Camões and together with his assistant, lifted Gem onto the examining table. I explained what had happened the previous night and he nodded slowly, checking her reflexes, and her eyes.

"I'm sorry to say, I think she has suffered a stroke. How old is she?"

"At least 14, we've had her for 12 years and we were told she was 18 months when we adopted her."

We both looked at her greying muzzle and at her back legs, always so muscled but now suddenly looking thin and wasted. She started to pant and seemed in some distress; I knew what was coming.

"I think she is in some pain now and with her age…I'm sorry but there is not a lot I can do."

"I understand. I knew when I brought her here."

"I can only give you my opinion, as the owner you must decide but if she were my dog…"

I couldn't stop the tears from sliding down my face but looking at her on the table, I knew I had no choice. My mantra is that if I can't give them a good life, I will give them a good death. Not in pain or fear but safe, warm and loved. She had made sure she accompanied us to Portugal and had seen us safely established here; she had done her job and I had to let her go.

"Yes, I give my permission," I said and she gently slipped away.

It's the hardest thing to do but every time there's a new puppy or kitten, a day like this will come around. For some, it's far in the future, for others, it's much nearer but it will come.

I drove home with tears streaming down my face, then gave Samson a huge hug. He looked lost too. Gem had always been there and now he had lost his friend and playmate. I wished I could explain to him.

I texted my mum and dad and Anne-Marie and called Edward, who rarely looked at text messages. Then, I had to call Nick. He was so shocked that it had all happened in the few days since he left but agreed it was for the best and although he enjoyed his time away, it was a difficult homecoming.

Our wedding anniversary is at the beginning of June and we all went out to our favourite Italian restaurant to celebrate. We had finished our meal by around 10.30, and it was a nice warm evening, so we decided to head to the terrace of one of our local bars for a nightcap. It's located in one of the narrow streets leading down to the beach; just a few parking spaces cut into the pavement, so cars could park facing in, at a slight angle. We pushed some tables together and made ourselves comfortable while deciding what to order.

Just as we settled, a car passed and pulled into one of the spaces but left its rear end sticking out into the road. The occupants all jumped out and hurried off before anyone could point it out to them. It caused a bit of a buzz of conversation around the tables, then everyone turned back to their meals and drinks. Jorge, the owner, came for a chat and to take our order, then as we waited, we heard a large coach approaching. As it got closer it became obvious that the parked car blocked the road and the coach wouldn't be able to pass.

The coach stopped just by our table, pumping out diesel fumes and beeped its horn. Normally, if you think you may have blocked someone in while running a quick errand, you listen for a car horn and rush back to move your vehicle, but not in this case. We had no idea where the occupants of the car had gone, it had Spanish plates so they must be on holiday and could have been in any number of restaurants or bars within walking distance, apparently, however, not in hearing distance.

The coach waited a few more minutes, then beeped again, louder and longer this time. Still, no one appeared. Other cars started coming down the road now and became blocked in behind the coach; the ones at the back started beeping their horns too. Five minutes passed, then ten. The coach driver grew more and more frustrated but there was nothing he could do. Suddenly, the doors opened and people started getting off the coach. The driver jumped down and opened the luggage compartment; a few people grabbed suitcases and started walking off into the village. We realised it must be an airport transfer bus dropping tourists off at their various hotels.

The driver went around to the front and weighed up whether he could make it through. Several of the customers at our bar shouted their opinions, the overwhelming one was that no, he wouldn't make it. He acknowledged the advice, shrugged and got back on the bus.

There were still quite a few people inside, probably going on to Ferragudo, Praia da Rocha, or Alvor, further along the coast. A few more minutes passed and one of the passengers got down and asked Jorge if he could use the toilets. Jorge showed him the way but when the guy came back out, instead of getting back on the bus, he sat down at a table and ordered a beer. The other passengers watched with interest and approval. A couple came and joined him, ordering a beer and a glass of wine. Next off, came a family of four, wanting a beer, a coffee and ice creams for the children. Slowly, the coach emptied and the bar filled up. The first guy had progressed to his second beer, accompanied by a large packet of crisps.

Someone called the police and the GNR arrived to direct the traffic. There was a small cut-through between the in and out roads, so they started to move some of the cars, sending them the wrong way through the cut-through, to alleviate the tailback. The driver finally cut the engine and came to join his passengers in the bar, just an orange juice for him, I noticed.

The family were now tucking into sandwiches and cakes and the bar was busier than I'd ever seen it at this time of night. From our vantage point, we could see past the coach and car and spotted who looked like the car's occupants walking up towards us. The driver speeded up, taking in the scene of the parked coach and the GNR vehicles with their lights flashing. He reached the car, jumped inside and attempted to reverse out of the space. Several others saw him at the same time and started shouting across to the GNR officers and pointing down the road. Two of the officers took off at a rate of knots and caught up with the car just as he was about to turn up a side road and escape. They blocked his path and opened the driver's door, motioning for him to get out. His passengers were now level with the car and watched as he was frogmarched back to the GNR vehicles for processing and no doubt receiving a large fine at the very least.

The coach driver drained his glass and got back on board, anxious to finish his shift. His passengers appeared slightly less enthusiastic; some had almost full drinks in front of them. He beeped the horn a final time and reluctantly, they drained their drinks, wrapped the remaining sandwiches in napkins, grabbed their crisps and got back on the coach. We had enjoyed the unexpected entertainment and Jorge's till looked a bit fuller than normal. The only loser I could see was the Spanish tourist.

For the last few months, every time I went into the local supermarket, they seemed to be playing the same song. It was a slow love song, by a singer with a voice like melted chocolate but I couldn't make out a title. I waited until the next time I heard it playing and approached one of the staff.

"This song, name?" I asked, pointing towards the ceiling, I don't know why.

The shop assistant looked upwards.

"Erm, song, cantar?"

I couldn't remember the word for song, the verb to sing would have to do.

"Oh, canção, sim."

"Comprar?" I knew the verb 'to buy' well enough.

She nodded and walked off towards the racks of CDs, flicking through them until she found it.

"É este."

She held out an album by a band called Santos e Pecadores. I added it to the items in my trolley and as soon as I had paid and loaded the shopping, I slid it into the CD player in the car. That beautiful voice again but I had to listen to several songs before the one I recognised came on. I checked the track list on the back of the CD case; it was called 'Fala-me de Amor' or 'Tell Me About Love'. I played it on repeat all the way home. Every time I was in the car on my own, going to or from a viewing, I would listen to the same CD over again, getting to like the rest of the songs just as much as Fala-me de Amor.

I was amazed to see a poster for the band a few weeks later; they were giving a free concert down by the quayside in Portimão, only 10-15 minutes away. I was determined we were going and convinced Nick, who had never heard of them, that it would be a good idea. The concert didn't start until 10 pm, so we had plenty of time to eat first and went to one of the seafood restaurants under the old bridge, within walking distance of the concert. The freshly grilled fish was delicious as usual, then we made our way down to the quayside. We passed the park with the queues at the ice cream kiosk; then the amusements assembled for the summer, a Ferris wheel and dodgem cars; finally, we saw the stage. The dark sky was clear and the neon lights danced in the river below.

A few people stood around the edge of the stage, but as the lights came on, looping and flashing and a backing track came to life, the audience grew. People appeared as if from nowhere as the beat got louder and stronger. Then silence, before a crash of drums and the members of the band hit the spotlight, going straight into their first number. The atmosphere was amazing; the open air, the dark sky, the bright lights and then pedestrians walking past as if it was an everyday occurrence to have a chart-topping band playing a free concert in a car park They played for over an hour. At the start of each song, I strained to hear the intro, but it was never my favourite. They announced the last track, still no luck.

"Obrigada, boa noite!" and they were gone. I had enjoyed the concert, but Fala-Me de Amor would have made it perfect. As we started to walk away, I heard those familiar chords. I'd thought it was too late for an encore but no, they were back, and they were playing my song.

One of the difficulties of living in Portugal, as we discovered, involved the never-ending bureaucracy; even the simplest of tasks could grow into something extremely complicated and time-consuming. The challenge affecting us and almost everyone at that time was the purchase of car tax or 'selo'. Everyone renewed their car tax at the same time, usually in June or July, but the exact dates changed each year and you had to watch for announcements in the newspapers and on TV. Once you knew the dates, you had to queue at the local Finanças office, the Junta de Freguesia, or even some newsagents, with your car registration documents, fiscal number, and payment.

I decided to go to the Junta de Freguesia in Carvoeiro but on my first attempt, I arrived at ten past two, only to find that they stopped issuing tax discs at two o'clock. I returned a few days later, barely a couple of days before the deadline produced the relevant documents and filled in the form, but this time they had run out of the correct tax discs for my car. I left my telephone number, expecting a call the next day to say they had more supplies, but then read in the Correio da Manhã newspaper that it was a national problem and the whole country had run out of 'selos', not just the Freguesia de Carvoeiro.

The situation became so bad that they had to extend the deadline for purchasing the 'selo' to the end of July. Following extremely long queues on the 31st, they extended it again to 14th August. I finally got a call and rushed straight to the Freguesia – before two o'clock – and came out clutching the precious stamp. Success at last and the car became legal again, at least until the next year.

We had had a busy few months at work but expected it to quieten down a bit in the summer as usual. However, my holiday rentals business reached fever pitch. Anne-Marie and Steve had asked me to deal with the bookings for their apartment too and recommended me to a couple of other owners on the development. Suddenly, I had a small portfolio of properties. Every lunchtime I rushed home and spent my break catching up on emails and sending out invoices. The booking forms came by post, and as internet banking wasn't that common, most people paid by cheque. I found it all very time-consuming, waiting for the postman, then going to the bank to deposit the payments. They were happy to accept sterling cheques but they took 21 working days to clear, and we took a risk on the exchange rate as the cheques were processed according to the rate on the day. I didn't meet all my clients, so I was also posting keys out and returning security deposits. It seems a very primitive system looking back on it now but we had come a long way from the classified ads in The Lady magazine.

One day, I arrived back for lunch at our little house. We used to leave the back door wedged open for the cats, but not wide enough for Samson to get out. I hurried back to let him out into the garden, while I set to work checking my emails for my second job. I could hear him barking but it didn't sound like his usual 'happy to be out, oh there's a bird' bark, more a concentrated, alert, type of bark. I went to the door to call him in and saw him standing by a shrub next to the sidewall. He was staring intently at something on the ground and emitting a single bark every few seconds.

"Samson, come on, that's enough now."

He completely ignored me and stayed rooted to the spot.

"Samson, SAMSON!"

Woof... woof... Woof.

"Come on, I've got work to do."

I went down the steps to get him, when I suddenly saw what was holding his attention, a tiny black and white kitten curled up under the shrub. This one was about 6 weeks old, not at all feral and not fazed by Samson either. It let me pick it up and just snuggled into my arms. I carried it inside and put it down on an armchair. I noticed it just stayed wherever I put it. The little thing looked quite dehydrated so I got some food and water and watched as it devoured everything. I spooned some more food into the dish and that soon disappeared too. It was a cute little thing but I wondered where it had come from. It definitely wasn't there when we left for work and the garden was so well enclosed. I began to wonder if someone deliberately followed us from house to house, dropping kittens for us to find?

It had finished eating and looked a bit perkier, so I picked it up again and checked the rear end, another girl by the looks of it. I decided to name her 'Minnie' as I had found her 'mooching' in the garden. Tink was showing quite an interest in our new arrival, so I put Minnie down next to her. They had a little sniff then Tink lifted one paw and smacked her right on top of her head. I decided she'd have to go into the bathroom while I went back to work, for her own safety. Plus, she could have a quiet snooze in there and rest and recuperate.

As I only worked on alternate days, I could take her for a health check the following day and after the usual flea and worm treatment, she had her first injection. We now had five cats.

16

The Next Move

In July and August, we only opened the office in the mornings; it was too hot to work in the afternoon, plus everyone was at the beach and not interested in viewing properties. I enjoyed having some extra downtime as, once again, we were starting to think about our next move. We had had enough of renting and not being able to unpack properly, buy our own furniture, or change things that didn't work for us. We really wanted to buy somewhere now that we were established, both busy with work and happy to stay in Carvoeiro.

The owner of the little house would be back in October, so we had to get our skates on to find somewhere we liked and be able to move by the end of September. We scoured the Portugal News and Algarve Resident every week and registered with every estate agent in the village but most properties were full of holiday rentals and wouldn't come up for sale until after the season had finished, too late for us.

In desperation, Nick started checking the classified ads of some of the national newspapers and spotted a small advert in the Correio de Manhã.

"Hey, listen to this. There's a one-bedroom, detached house, with a garden, walking distance of Carvoeiro. What are the chances of that, in a national paper?"

"Really, how much?"

"They're asking 195.000 euros and maybe they'll take an offer."

"That sounds like a good price, is there a contact number?"

"Yes, it looks like a private sale. I'll give them a call."

I stayed nearby in case it was a Portuguese owner who didn't speak English, but I needn't have worried. Nick was soon chatting away so I left him to it and took my book out to the garden. I just heard the end of the conversation as he came down the steps towards me.

"...yes fine, ok, I know it, 3 pm tomorrow, thanks, see you then."

He ended the call and grinned.

"It belongs to an English guy but he's spending more time in Lisbon now with his business, and we can go and see it tomorrow."

"Does it sound interesting?"

"Yes, it does, unique really. He says it was built as the sales office for a small development of detached villas, then when they were all sold, it was converted into a house. Plus, he's had plans drawn up to put in a first floor with another bedroom and bathroom."

"Oh, that sounds intriguing!" I couldn't wait for the next afternoon.

We followed the directions and found ourselves driving past our previous rental. It was strange to see it full of holidaymakers sitting on 'our' balcony and hearing them diving into the swimming pool that had never been warm enough for us to jump into.

"I wonder how they like all the surface pipework?" mused Nick.

"I wonder how they're getting on with Maria."

Just around the corner, we found our potential new home. The gate stood wide open so we walked in, past a row of small palm trees. On the wall behind, we saw the name of the development.

Tom appeared from the rear of the house.

"Hi, you found it ok?"

"Yes, no problem. We actually used to live just around the corner."

"Oh, that's handy, so you know the area?"

"Yes, we spent six months there before we moved to our current place. We're renting at the moment, but ready to buy somewhere permanent now."

"Have you been in Portugal long?"

"It will be a year in October, but we've been visiting for the last 15 years or so."

"Ah ok," said Tom. "I've been here about 10 years now, between here and Lisbon."

We'd noticed there was always a bit of competition when two or more ex-pats met, a little good-humoured jostling for position, as to who had been here the longest. We were newbies but couldn't help adding in our years of holidays, trying to establish our connection with the place. Now we're old hands, coming up for 20 years of residence, and I've even taken Portuguese citizenship so we don't meet too many who have been here longer than us anymore.

Tom started to explain about the house and we followed him on the tour, entering via the back door and into the kitchen. The first thing we noticed, the house formed almost a full circle; the second, the kitchen had no windows.

A single lightbulb hung from the middle of the ceiling and facing us a wall with a sink, hob and some wall and floor cabinets. Tom opened one to show us the gas water heater. To our left, stood a small table with a microwave on top and beside it, a fridge/freezer. In the middle of the room, we found a dining table and chairs.

"Well, this is the kitchen. I don't really spend that much time here so it does me fine." He looked around as if seeing it through our eyes. "I'm sure you could make a lot more of it."

"Yes, there's lots of, er, potential," said Nick.

"Yes, I agreed, lots," I said, looking sadly at the dull, dark floor tiles and yellow-painted walls.

"Ok, there's a little corridor through here."

He wasn't joking, there was barely room for the three of us.

"And this is the living room."

We passed through some bizarre, Wild West type saloon shutters. This looked more promising. The outside wall was curved, with four large windows set into it, letting in plenty of light. I was getting to like the quirkiness, especially the curved walls. It also had a log burner, another tick.

Tom pulled back a curtain to reveal another windowless room.

"This wall here," he said, slapping his hand on yet another curved wall that cut across the living room, from the curtain to the outside wall, beside the log burner, "this used to be the reception desk when I bought it. It was about waist high but I built it up to the ceiling to make a bedroom for my son, who comes over for the holidays sometimes."

"Do you think we could take it down?" asked Nick.

"Yes, I'm sure you could, it's not a supporting wall or anything, cos it was only ever the desk. I think it would be quite an easy job."

It would be quite a messy job, I thought, but it would make the room much bigger, or maybe we could keep it as my office. I realised I was starting to see us in this funny little house and the potential existed to make it into something much more comfortable than at present. We shuffled back into the corridor and as in the little house at Algar Seco, once again we could see into all the rooms from this little space.

"This is the bedroom," said Tom, indicating a small room to the left. "Opposite is the bathroom."

We peered inside, it looked in need of re-tiling, but functional.

"And here's the storeroom."

Tom tried to open the door a few inches but we could see it was piled high with boxes and plastic sacks.

"Oh, that's handy for storage," I said, pleased to be able to compliment something at last.

"It's actually another loo but I had all the fittings taken out and made into a normal room."

"It could be turned back into a bathroom?" I asked. Now, this sounded interesting.

"Yes, all the pipes and drains are still there, just tiled over. You see, when this was an office, they had a ladies and a gents. The ladies' loo was converted into the bathroom and this was the gents."

I could cope with one bedroom but I'd cope even better if we had two bathrooms. The possibilities were just piling on now.

Tour over, we went back out into the garden. It was dusty and full of spindly pine trees that had grown far too tall, mostly just trunks with a few leaves on the very top branches. They would have to come down. But I noticed some beautiful hibiscus planted down one boundary, absolutely covered in deep red flowers, and the garden looked secure for Samson, with high walls on two sides and a solid fence on the other. We took a last look around and went off to have a chat about it, assuring Tom we would be in touch. We had a quick walk around the area. It seemed quiet, with lots of much larger houses and a big bonus, a lot of open land for walking Samson. And I was sure we would be looking to get another dog once we were settled.

As soon as we were back in the car, we both started talking at once.

"…re-instate the bathroom."

"…take that wall down."

We stopped and started laughing. We were both as keen as each other and bursting with ideas.

"You know, I think we could make something of that house," said Nick.

"I do too. We've been fine in the little house all summer; it's not such an issue when you spend more time outside in this climate and it will be easier to heat in winter. And we don't have to do all the work at once. I think we should put in an offer."

We didn't want to seem too keen, but we didn't want to lose it either. Nick decided to sound Tom out. It didn't go too well.

"I don't think he's prepared to come down on the price. He said he's taken into account that by selling privately and not paying an estate agent, we're already saving that money. And the worst of it is, that he's not 100% sure he wants to sell."

"Why advertise it, if he doesn't want to sell?"

I could see our dreams and plans disappearing rapidly.

"He was just testing the market, thinking maybe a Lisbon couple would want it as a weekend bolt hole but he didn't expect anyone so quickly."

"Oh, I hope he doesn't change his mind; there's nothing else on the market that is as perfect for us."

"I know, he said he'll have a think and let us know in a few days."

I hated this feeling of being in limbo, I much prefer to know what I'm dealing with, good or bad, but not knowing was killing me. I'd just have to be patient; not one of my strong points.

We put the house to the back of our minds and tried to enjoy the summer but it was now August and with most of the estate agents closed, or barely open, we started looking for another rental. Whatever happened, we had to be out in a couple of months and now we had a dog and five cats. it would be even more of a struggle to find somewhere.

The heat was more than we had experienced before. Although we had already visited in most months, we had never been in July and August. We were all feeling it, even Samson wasn't his usual self. Normally he'd get up ready for his walk around 8 am, while the temperatures felt still bearable, then home for breakfast. Gradually, we noticed he was less keen on going out and not that fussed about his food either. We reassured each other that it was just the heat and made sure he had fans and a cool mat to lie on, but day by day, he got worse so we made another trip up to Carlos, the vet.

After a full examination, he seemed a little perplexed.

"The blood results are more or less ok, a little high on the liver, but not too bad, but I hear something in the heart and maybe lungs. I'll try him with a diuretic, there may be some fluid on the lungs. Come back in three days."

We took him home and gave him the medication but he still refused to go for a walk and wouldn't even eat his favourite sardines in tomato sauce.

Back at the clinic, Carlos could see that he hadn't improved, and in fact was a little bit worse than before.

"I think I'll take an x-ray, just to see what is happening."

We waited outside for about twenty minutes, then his assistant called us back in.

"I can still see fluid on the lungs, but I think I should send you to the Veterinary Hospital in Loulé; their machine is much better, makes better pictures."

He picked up the phone and dialled the hospital, speaking to a colleague there. He put his hand over the receiver.

"Can you go now?"

"Yes, of course, do they think they can help Samson?" Nick asked.

Carlos shrugged.

"I hope so but first they need to see him."

He spoke into the receiver again, nodding while he listened to the reply. He replaced the receiver and started scribbling on a pad on his desk. He held the paper out to Nick.

"Here is the address; it is very easy to find. They are expecting you and will call me as soon as they have made the tests."

We thanked him and rushed out to the car, anxious to get there as soon as possible. Carlos didn't seem too hopeful and I had a bad feeling as we drove along to Loulé.

As soon as we arrived, they took Samson off for tests. We sat in the waiting room, glad of the aircon and the water cooler. We had left home that morning expecting a quick trip to the vet and hadn't thought to bring any food or water with us.

The vet reappeared and called us into the consulting room. Samson was lying on the table, his breathing seemed fast and shallow.

"We have taken some x-rays and some blood, and I'm sorry to say the lungs, they are completely covered in tumours." He turned to place the x-rays on the lightboxes. "You see these white patches, here, and here?" he circled them with his pen, "these are tumours, I think secondary tumours, we don't know where is the primary site, but possibly the liver or spleen."

As he spoke, I looked at Samson. Suddenly I could see it in his eyes and feel it under my hand as I stroked his side. I couldn't believe I was here again so soon after Gem. Samson was only 8, I thought we'd have another good four or five years with him. I couldn't lose him; I'd never been without a dog in my whole life.

The vet carried on speaking but I wasn't listening now. I knew what he was going to say; but maybe if I didn't hear it, it wouldn't be true. Nick took my hand; his hand was shaking and I could hear his breathing was shaky too, he was trying to hold back the tears.

I watched as they shook hands and Nick picked Samson up to carry him to the car. Once he was settled, I asked what the vet had recommended.

"He spoke to Carlos and explained that we have to meet him back at the clinic now."

"Now?" I looked at my watch, all sense of time had gone, it had seemed to stand still while we were in the waiting room. "But it's four o'clock; it's Saturday, Carlos closes at one on Saturdays."

"He's going to meet us there; he's coming back in for us, for Samson."

"Is this it?" Not yet, I thought, not today. I wasn't ready.

"Yes, he's suffering now, there's nothing else they can do, we don't have a choice."

We drove back in silence, punctuated with sobs.

Carlos stood waiting for us, a gruff, middle-aged vet who'd seen it all, standing at the clinic door with tears in his eyes, while we said goodbye to Samson.

The house felt so empty; we gathered up the dog leads, beds and bowls. No need to rush home to let them out, or take them for walks. We both felt bereft. I'd never been without a dog and Nick had got one as soon as he left home, Sabre, his beloved German Shepherd. Our first dates were taking our family dog, Shayla, a flat coat retriever, and Sabre out on country walks. Dogs were so much a part of us and now we didn't have any. It took a while to sink in.

But life had to go on and later that week, we had some good news, at last, Tom was definitely selling the house, and selling it to us. We made an appointment with the lawyer who had handled the purchase of the apartment and started the ball rolling, hoping for a completion date before the end of

September.

In the middle of August, the FATACIL (Feira de Artesanato, Turismo, Agricultura, Comércio e Indústria de Lagoa) opened. The biggest annual event in Lagoa ran for 10 days every year and resembled an English County Show with a mixture of trade stands, craft stalls and opportunities to try traditional food and drinks. It also had horse and dog shows, as well as livestock on display.

I found the craft stands especially interesting, with beautiful stained glass, woven baskets, wood carvings, pottery, lace embroidery and items made from cork. Each night, live music hit the stage next to the open-air restaurants and on this particular year, the crowds thrilled to, amongst others, Kalulu, Xutos e Pontapés and Boney M! Hundreds of cars parked up along the N125 every night as crowds arrived from all over the surrounding area, even though you could park in the official car parks for just two euros.

Coinciding with the end of Fatacil, came the local festival of Nossa Senhora de Encarnação. The festivities lasted all weekend with activities for the children on the beach, and a 'goodbye to summer party' on Saturday evening, with DJs and dancing until the early hours. We visited Fatacil on Sunday, then went into Carvoeiro for the Nossa Senhora de Encarnação procession, and managed to get seats at our usual vantage point on the terrace of Matabixo. The upstairs bar faced the square and the beach, giving a perfect view of the procession which consisted of the Priest leading a marching band, followed by a large statue of Nossa Senhora (Our Lady) set on a plinth, decorated with flowers, and carried by six men. It came down from the church, along the 'out' road, then back down the 'in' road, across the square and back up the hill to the church. Around midnight, the firework display signified the end of the festival - and the end of summer.

17

January 2009, Lisbon, Intensive Care

"Boa noite, obrigado,"

I opened my eyes, what had I just heard? 'Thank you, good night?'

"What time is it?" I asked.

"Dez da noite."

Ten at night? What on earth…?

"Don't worry, we have spoken to your husband. He knows everything, he is waiting outside."

How could it be ten at night? I could tell I was still in the operating theatre. What happened to my 5-hour operation?

"We're just waiting for an intensive care bed for you. Don't worry, everything's fine."

What happened to no intensive care?

I was lying flat on my back with a feeding tube up my nose, cannulas in the back of each hand and in each wrist, a central port with 2 or 3 tubes going into my neck and a raging thirst. The nurse placed a damp sponge to my lips; they were cracked and dry, but the tiny amount of water I was allowed only made me thirstier.

A porter arrived and I was whisked out through the double doors and into the corridor outside. I heard footsteps approaching the trolley and saw Nick staring down at me, looking a bit shocked. I had so many questions but I found it difficult to speak, and anyway we were hurtling along the corridor. Then the porter manoeuvred my trolley, plus various drips and machines, into a lift.

Up one floor to the ICU which looked very different from what I had imagined. He parked me in a bay, with the bed-head raised slightly, so I could have a look around the room. All the patients lay arranged in a semi-circle, each surrounded by a bank of machines beeping and pumping away. The centre of the room contained several rows of desks with doctors and nurses working at computer screens, in between checking on their patients. The room felt brightly lit and quite noisy. I had expected it to be calm with dimmed lights, but it could have been 10 in the morning rather than 11 at night.

My mouth felt dry, my throat raw, I couldn't move at all. They let Nick stay for half an hour, and just as he was getting ready to leave, the doors swung open and my surgeon swept in. He looked so fresh and energetic, not at all like someone who had been in theatre for 14 hours, performing a particularly difficult surgery. He waved a brown envelope and smiled broadly.

"Do you want to see some pictures?" he asked, head on one side.

Before I could answer. he slid two black x-rays out of the envelope and held them up, one in each hand, with an air of triumph. One showed my spine from the front, the other from the side. It looked straighter than it had been, but still bore a definite curve and was now held in place by titanium rods and screws, vertical and horizontal, like an internal scaffold. The rods went from between my shoulder blades right down to the bottom of my spine. Eight vertebrae were now fused and immobile.

"Look, look!" he exclaimed. "Doesn't it look good? It's even better than I thought it would be. You have very good value from this surgery," he grinned. "Ten thousand euros of titanium."

He waved his hand across the x-ray with a flourish, as if displaying the prizes on a TV show. I don't think I gave him the reaction he expected; he clearly felt extremely pleased with himself. Slightly crestfallen, he dropped the x-rays onto a nearby table and approached my bed. He checked the cannulas and drips, then without warning, took his pen out of the top pocket of his white coat and drew it up the soles of my feet. I yelped.

"Excellent!" he grinned.

He slapped Nick on the back, turned on his heel and with a wave, disappeared through the door, shouting:

"See you tomorrow!"

"Oh well, if things get tough I can always weigh you in for scrap." Nick murmured.

I was fairly well drugged up so the next 24 hours were a blur of strange faces and even stranger noises. The room appeared a constant bustle of activity, beds moved in and out, samples collected and results brought back. The lights never dimmed and I lost all track of time. I asked for a glass of water but was only allowed a small sip. They told me they could only remove the nasal-gastric tube, once they knew I wasn't going to throw up. I felt no pain and just floated away, never sure if I was asleep or awake or somewhere in between.

Suddenly, I felt a jolt and saw a face close to mine; a nurse explained that I was being moved back down to the normal ward and how pleased they were, that I'd done so well. I couldn't recall doing anything but accepted her congratulations. I was looking forward to being back in my room with the view of the 25th April bridge and my mani-pedi friend.

Back on the ward, it felt like weeks had passed, not just over 24 hours. Normality seemed strange; visitors passed wearing normal clothes instead of surgical scrubs. We sped along and I realised we had already passed my room but I couldn't get the porter's attention. We turned left and left again and came to a halt. A team of staff surrounded my bed and made preparations to slide me into my new home. I felt sure they'd made a mistake but they chatted away amongst themselves, tucked me in, closed the curtains around me and left.

A friendly face appeared; the nurse slid through the curtains and checked my nameplate.

"Karen?" she attempted.

It's a very unusual name in Portugal and originally, they didn't even have a letter K in the alphabet, c and q providing all the K sounds. It was only added to allow for foreign words, like Karen.

The nurse introduced herself as Fatima and it became obvious that she spoke no English at all. Now my Portuguese was ok at this point, but I had never needed 'hospital Portuguese' before, so I thought this might prove interesting. Fatima checked all my drips and started to remove some, explaining as she went. I understood the majority of it. Then she checked my temperature and blood pressure and was satisfied that I'd been handed over in an acceptable condition.

I now became aware of something else; it appeared that while I'd been in theatre, they'd taken the opportunity to catheterise me, one of the things I had been dreading. She checked the bag and changed it very efficiently and with a complete lack of embarrassment, chatting away all the time. When eventually the time came for it to be removed, I actually missed it.

I came to realise that I represented an object of curiosity, as the only non-Portuguese in the hospital. I got used to answering the same questions over and over: how long had I lived in Portugal? Why had I come to live here? Why had I left the UK? This last question seemed to puzzle everyone the most. Portugal was still reeling from the effects of the global credit crunch and austerity appeared everywhere you looked. Plus, there had been a general slowdown and recession since the early 2000s so it had hit the country particularly hard.

Just about everyone I came into contact with expressed amazement that we preferred to live in Portugal, rather than in the UK. They thought of our country as the land of milk and honey with plentiful jobs and incredibly high salaries. They all seemed to know someone, a niece or cousin, who had moved to the UK and was earning more than they could have hoped for at home. At the time, the minimum wage stood at around 500€ per month. I tried to explain the relatively high cost of living in the UK and that we had moved for a better quality of life and a slower pace, but they just looked at me as if I lacked all common sense and shook their heads sadly at my ignorance.

Although I always found the Portuguese extremely friendly and welcoming, I also soon realised how completely honest and direct they could be. They had no problem pointing out that you'd put on weight or looked tired. I had had my hair cut extremely short, knowing that I would be virtually bedbound for a lot of my recovery and I thought it would make life much easier. This meant that all the dye had also gone and the nurses and ancillary staff stared at me and asked:

"Why don't you paint your hair?"

My explanation didn't seem to satisfy them as very few would consider giving in to grey hair in their 40s, 50s or even 70s. My skin tone was also fair game, once I was allowed to shower.

"You're very white," said the nurse, looking me up and down, not in a nasty way, or as an insult, just as a statement of fact.

It was January and I couldn't help but agree with her; the summer seemed a long time ago.

They put me back in a 2-bed ward, but so far, I hadn't seen or heard anything of my neighbour. I was still flat on my back unable to move and nurses came to turn me every couple of hours, but that didn't include my head, so I could only stare at the ceiling. I heard the staff talking to a 'Dona Ana' but couldn't hear her replies so had no idea how old she was or what operation she had had. We only had a tiny window, looking on to another part of the hospital and the weather appeared wet and miserable; the hospital, on the other hand, felt stiflingly hot.

Dona Ana was nearer the window and seemed to feel the cold as they kept bringing her extra blankets, whereas I was boiling. I have never liked my feet being 'trapped' under bed clothes but every time my bed was made the ends were tucked in, which felt so claustrophobic. It was another thing I had to explain and which made me sound like some sort of madwoman. It also made the room look untidy without hospital corners but they indulged my weird ways and it became a bit of a joke.

As promised, Theo arrived to see me, wearing a huge Drizabone coat and wide-brimmed hat which dripped all over me. He had a chat with the nurse on duty and a few words with me, then out came the pen again to check the soles of my feet; at least he appreciated the easy access of non-tucked in sheets.

No sooner had he left, than I could hear the clanking of food trolleys advancing down the corridor, accompanied by the theme tune to the Portuguese version of The Price is Right, a national institution, televised every night and avidly watched by millions. The TV was in a lounge area along the corridor, so we couldn't watch but just heard the programmes. It was set to maximum volume and never got adjusted down. I became quite adept at guessing the programme, although wildlife programmes presented an issue as they had more music than speech, so if I missed the introduction, I was lost.

The trolley stopped outside our room and a cheerful, smiling auxiliary came in carrying two trays, expecting me to sit up to eat.

"No problem," she said when I explained.

She produced the over-bed, wheelie table, which came just about level with my chin. Just then Nick appeared for visiting time and he cut my food up for me and helped me to spear a piece of fish. It looked very similar to the meal I'd had the night before my op, the same cauliflower à la Dettol. Pudding was an orange, also not ideal when you're flat on your back. We were just about to give up on my dinner when 4 people came into the room and walked around to Dona Ana's bed. We assumed they were her husband and children, if so, she had to be around 65-70. They all chatted away to her and I could hear her replies now. She sounded quite frail and tired but her family were a fairly lively bunch and in typical Portuguese style, I found it hard to work out if they were having a normal discussion or an argument. Also, in typical Portuguese style, they very politely acknowledged us, when they arrived and left.

After our visitors had gone and the nurses finished their rounds, we were finally left in peace for a short time, although the TV still blared away with some kind of news or current affairs programme. Lots of heated voices seemed involved in an argument, which I had absolutely no chance of understanding as they interrupted and spoke over each other, much the same as similar UK programmes.

I was still flat on my back, unable to see Dona Ana, and also still reliant on the staff turning me every few hours. Anything just slightly out of reach on my tray or table may as well have been miles away. I didn't like to keep pressing the call button as the nurses were obviously kept busy enough. I heard them swish past attending to patients who sounded much worse than I felt. Suddenly I heard a sound, a croaky whisper:

"Olá senhora, como está?"

It felt quite surreal, having a conversation with someone I had never seen, but we managed to chat for an hour or so. I heard all about her family, how old they were, where they worked and as I had seen them all file in and out, I could identify each of her four children, aged between 35 and 47. Dona Ana was walking towards 70 as the Portuguese put it, and lived in Sintra, just outside Lisbon. She was surprised that I was British and that I lived in the Algarve.

"Why would you want to live there?" she asked, "it's almost Morocco."

She did acknowledge that my Portuguese was quite good, in spite of my Algarvean accent. She asked all about my surgery and explained that she had twice had operations on a tumour on her spine; it wasn't life-threatening, but could cause paralysis if left unchecked. Her treatment had gone well but it had left her with very low blood pressure, the reason she was still in hospital. Every time she tried to get out of bed, she fainted. The conversation had tired me out, so I wished her good night and tried to sleep. Being used to sleeping on my side I found it difficult to nod off but I must have done as the next thing I knew, the breakfast trolley clanked into the room.

I was surprised to find that breakfast consisted of just coffee and a roll with butter or jam. No menus arrived for us to tick as in UK hospitals; breakfast remained the same every day, and lunch and dinner were meat or fish. I was pescatarian so every meal was fish, more often than not a whole, un-filleted one, as served up the previous evening. I could see this was going to be a challenge. I called Nick from my mobile and asked him to bring me some snacks that I would find easy to manage in my current situation and later that afternoon he came in laden with several carrier bags.

We had planned for him to go home in a couple of days, leaving me on my own until he came back up to collect me, once I knew when I was being discharged. This presented a problem that we couldn't find a solution to. We couldn't return by train, or by bus, and didn't want Nick driving into the centre of Lisbon, then straight back home, a round trip of at least 6 hours, not including any waiting for medication etc at the hospital. We could have requested an ambulance but that would mean travelling back with several other people, not knowing if we'd be dropped home first or last; the journey could have taken all day. It was really worrying us both because we just couldn't see any way around it.

After breakfast, two women bustled in, weighed down with clean bedding and various bowls containing flannels and soaps. They set to work, filling the basins with warm water, chatting away to each other and Dona Ana, nodding and smiling at me. I heard Dona Ana explain that my Portuguese was ok, so one of them approached me with a basin full of soapy water and a towel over her arm. I had no idea what to expect. Surely, she knew I couldn't get out of bed? I started to explain, but she smiled and shook her head. Ah, apparently, she had come to give me my first ever bed bath. I felt mortified. I thought I had covered all the potentially humiliating situations but this hadn't occurred to me at all. I protested that I was fine, but she refused to take no for an answer and applied the soapy flannel with a speedy, but very efficient, hand.

I hadn't realised how grubby I'd felt; after all, 48 hours had elapsed since my pre-op shower. And actually, I felt much better once she'd finished and I'd put my arms through a clean hospital gown, there was no point in doing it up as I still wasn't going anywhere. After the bed bath, they rolled me onto one side, whipped away the sheet below me and replaced it. In no time both I and my bed felt clean and fresh. Nothing like a clean bed.

Dona Ana's family arrived promptly for visiting time again. Ignoring the two visitors to a bed rule, not only were all four children in attendance, plus her husband, they'd also brought another couple with them. I never established whether they were friends or family, as again the chatter was too fast for me to follow, but I noticed them passing around Pasteís de Nata, the custard tarts that Portugal and particularly Lisbon are famous for. In fact, the bakery which claimed to be the original supplier of Pastéis de Nata stood almost next door to the hospital and I recognised their name on the white cardboard box. They're renowned for their pastries and are supposed to be the best in Portugal.

Suddenly, the box appeared around my curtain and with customary Britishness, I declined the kind offer, although I felt really intrigued to try one. However, as the Portuguese generally say what they mean and mean what they say, they expect the same from you, so the box was whipped away just as quickly and I saw the last custard tart picked up and demolished without a second glance in my direction. I could have kicked myself – except I couldn't.

Saturday night proved a long one. Not only were my opiate painkillers being withdrawn, but it was also a busy night in Lisbon, with a never-ending stream of sirens, coming closer and closer and I knew they were heading for the hospital. I had no idea what had occurred but some of the injured were brought up to my ward and I could hear crying and weeping from either patients or relatives, I couldn't tell which. Obviously, some people had come in extremely ill. Alarms sounded and the night staff ran to treat the most serious cases. Chaos reigned and through it all I had very vivid dreams and nightmares, not knowing what was real and what was my imagination.

I felt so relieved when the lights snapped on and the now-familiar clanking of the breakfast trolley came down the corridor. Another roll and jam, another bed bath and clean sheets, I was getting into the routine now, and the nursing and auxiliary staff chatted to me as much as Dona Ana. I was surprised that I could follow all their conversation. I learnt what they had watched on TV the previous night, what they cooked for dinner, what mischief their children, or husbands, had been up to; I gathered a lot of very useful vocabulary.

The day followed the old familiar pattern, until visiting time came around and Nick arrived, closely followed by my parents who had made the 3-hour journey on the train, even though my dad had recently had major surgery himself. It was a lovely surprise to see them and we had a couple of hours to chat, knowing that we could discuss everyone and everything quite openly, as no one else on the ward spoke or understood any English. I think I may have been the only 'Estrangeira' in the whole hospital.

Mum and dad had booked a room in the same hotel as Nick, which boasted a rooftop restaurant with views over the centre of Lisbon. Did I envy them their delicious meal and spectacular views, as a whole fish and Dettol vegetables arrived before me? I felt exhausted, but my visitors had definitely made the day pass more quickly and had come armed with more snacks, so I settled down for a quiet night.

Monday morning dawned with an air of back to business, everyone seemed slightly more organised and efficient. There had been no doctors' rounds over the weekend, but now I faced a continuous queue of nurses, junior doctors and physiotherapists, who explained the plan for me, for the day and the coming week. Apparently, I was going to get out of bed. I had absolutely no idea how I would achieve this as I was still unable to even turn over on my own. I would also have my dressing changed, which meant I'd be able to have a proper shower and wash my hair before a new dressing was applied, and I would walk down to the showers at the other end of the corridor. I found this all quite overwhelming, I had got used to having everything brought to me and done for me, and now I had to start taking baby steps, literally, on the way back to living a normal life. I dropped off to sleep, shattered at the thought of it all.

I woke up to see Nick and my parents standing by the bed. They had special permission to visit early so they could get the afternoon train home. We just had time for a quick chat and an update on my busy day, when they had to leave to meet our lovely tame taxi driver, who was booked to take them back to the station. Nick had arranged to meet him at the front entrance, quite a few minutes' walk from the ward, so they set off and I waited for someone to come and start the promised dressing removal and shower plan.

An unfamiliar man appeared in the doorway, looked around anxiously, then beamed when he saw me. I assumed he was a member of staff and I was just pondering his lack of uniform when he rushed forward and placed his hand on mine.

"Ah senhora, como está?" he said.

"Bem obrigada," I replied, still wondering who he was.

Suddenly, I recognised his voice - our taxi driver, who had arrived early and trawled the hospital looking for 'the English lady with the back'. While he continued explaining, I was on the wrong track altogether and tried to tell him that Nick and my parents were waiting for him at the front entrance.

"Don't worry," he said, patting my hand. "I'm going there now. I just came to see how you are. You look very well, good luck, get well soon, 'as melhores," and he slipped out the door.

Dona Ana had obviously been eavesdropping and was curious about my visitor. I explained he was the taxi driver who had brought us from the station and come to take my parents back there. I could hear her murmur approvingly, no less than she'd expect from a Lisboeta!

A male nurse appeared, with a tray of instruments and various bottles and jars. He introduced himself and explained that I was going for a shower and afterwards, he would change my dressing and check the scar. Just then a female auxiliary arrived and the time had come for me to get out of bed. She threw back the covers; I looked at my legs and then at the floor. I didn't know what to do; how would I manoeuvre my feet onto the tiles? Dona Ana called out words of encouragement from the sidelines but I still couldn't work it out. I had completely forgotten how to get out of bed.

Fatima, the auxiliary, tried to help, rolling me onto my side and offering her arm for me to pull myself up on, but I didn't know what to do with my arms, which one went where? I felt genuinely confused. The male nurse, Marco, came over to see what was taking so long. I looked at him helplessly.

"I don't know how to get up," I bleated.

He lowered the bed, so the gap wasn't so daunting and moved my legs to the edge. As he pulled me up by my arms, Fatima pushed my legs down to the floor and suddenly I found myself sitting on the edge. They took an arm each to support me and up I went, I was standing. It was such a strange feeling after so many days in bed and I felt very wary of bending or twisting the wrong way. Then I discovered that I couldn't bend or twist anymore, and the way I had just got out of bed would be the way I'd have to do it for the rest of my life. The combination of being upright and the realisation of the magnitude of how much my life had changed, made me feel nauseous and dizzy, and it was lucky that Marco and Fatima were holding me up or I'd have crashed to the floor. My knees buckled and I just wanted to get back into my safe haven, but we had only just started the procedure.

Fatima turned to face me and put both my hands on her shoulders. Walking backwards, she started to guide me out of the room. Just putting one foot in front of the other seemed as impossible as running a marathon, but she persisted; I had to start moving or I'd lose muscle tone which would make my recovery even harder. We turned the corner and out into the corridor. I could see the shower room at the end, at least a mile away, but inch by inch we drew closer and my legs started to remember how to walk.

The shower room was fully kitted out for disabled patients, with handrails and emergency pull cords. Fatima removed my gown and sat me on a stool under the warm water, and left me to wash and shampoo my hair, as best I could. I'd been dreading it, but actually, it felt like bliss and surprisingly I had no pain at all. After a few minutes, she reappeared with a towel and clean gown and helped me to dry and dress before we set off on our slow journey back.

Dona Ana clapped excitedly to see me return.

"Well done!" she called out and for the first time, I saw her face.

Marco also looked pleased to see me back. He was all gloved up ready for his star performance. I had the same reaction when it came to lying back down on the bed, with no idea how to achieve it. Marco and Fatima helped me to sit down on the edge of the bed, then simultaneously swung my legs up as I lowered myself down on one elbow, in a sort of pendulum motion. This way I could keep my spine straight, then roll gently onto my back. I still have to use this method now, 12 years later and for the rest of my life.

I rolled onto my other side and Marco started to remove the dressing, he was extremely pleased with how it was healing. I asked how many stitches I had and he tutted.

"They are staples; stitches inside, staples outside." He counted them. "I think around 32."

More than I thought, but good news, no sign of any infection or problems with the surgery, so he was happy to re-dress the scar and he did it so gently and carefully that I didn't feel a thing, just relief that everything had gone to plan so far. The wound had been checked and my legs worked. An element of doubt had always hung in the air; even the great maestro himself admitted to never having performed this surgery before, neither as extensively nor on someone of my advanced age, 43; scoliosis surgery is normally performed on late teenagers. He had given no guarantees; the only thing he said was that without the surgery, I'd be heading for a wheelchair very soon.

I felt shattered after my exertions, but the lunch trolley soon battered its way down the corridor, and just as I finished my usual fish and Dettol, my physiotherapist appeared, all bright and breezy, in the time-honoured way of all hospital physios.

"Right," she said. "Are we ready to get moving?"

I groaned, I thought I might at least have the rest of the day off, but no, in she came, wheeling the wheelchair and positioned it beside my bed. I tried to protest but she whipped the covers off me, then hesitated. I was still just wearing a backless gown, with my arms pushed through the sleeves, not exactly suitable for physiotherapy. She held up her index finger.

"Wait there a moment," she said and disappeared around the

corner.

Where did she think I could go to? She swiftly returned, accompanied by Fatima, carrying arm-fulls of nightwear. I had brought my own nightdress but, after inspecting it, they deemed it unsuitable. Fatima then proceeded to display all the options available, as if I was choosing a new ballgown in some designer atelier. I could have large blue and white striped pyjamas, large brown and white pyjamas, or, an attractive set of large, faded and faintly stained, grey and white pyjamas – all of them men's. I decided on the blue and white, fresher looking and showed off my eyes.

Fatima helped me into them, they were enormous, the jacket would have gone around me at least 3 times, and the cord at the waist of the bottoms had to be tied in several knots but hey, they gave plenty of room for movement, and at least my modesty would be preserved, so we were good to go. We had another practice of the pendulum movement to get me upright, then all three of us transferred me to the wheelchair.

This was a new experience, not helped by the fact that it only had one footrest, so I wasn't sure what to do with my left foot. Should I hold it up clear of the floor, or squash it next to the right foot, happily supported by the only footrest? Neither Fatima nor the physio commented on the missing footrest and as I travelled around the hospital towards the physiotherapy department, I became slightly obsessed with checking all the wheelchairs we came across. Not one had both footrests; obviously, the hospital equivalent of the mystery of the missing socks in the laundry, although how you can fail to notice all the footrests falling off, I don't know.

The physiotherapy room was huge, with windows stretching

along the whole length of one wall, with a fascinating close-up view of the 25th April Bridge, even closer than it had been in my first room. The cars seemed to be heading straight at us but the bridge curved at the last minute and they sped away past the corner of the room. It was kitted out with all manner of equipment, parallel bars, crash mats, chairs of different shapes and sizes, weights, bean bags and at least half a dozen staff putting patients through their paces. It appeared that some had suffered strokes or other types of head injury, others looked like they had survived fairly nasty road accidents, including one or two amputees, but all were busy, intent on their given tasks and hoping for as good a recovery as possible.

They wheeled me to an area with several thick foam cushions placed on top of each other and we practised the 'log roll' to get in and out of bed. That went pretty well, but when we progressed to sitting and standing, things deteriorated. The physio insisted on making me go from standing to sitting with my feet together, which I found physically impossible as I had to turn one foot at an angle to achieve it. This didn't go down well; after half an hour of trying, I had to call it a day. I needed a rest and asked if I could go back to the ward. I must have looked a bit grey as she agreed and wheeled me back, both feet clinging to the single footrest. I have still never mastered sitting down with my feet together, it makes for a fairly unladylike descent, but it's the only way I can achieve it now.

I knew Nick's evening visit would be his last for a while; we had agreed that once I was over the worst, he would return home to check on all our animals and catch up on some work, then return on my release date. That brought the issue of how I would get home back into focus. However, while he filleted my fish and Dettol, I had the germ of an idea, what about our tame taxi driver? He had volunteered to help in any way he could; it was January and he had already told us this was a quiet time for the taxis, with few tourists around. We had no idea how much he would charge or whether he would even be interested but Nick went outside to call him anyway, it was worth asking.

He came back with a big grin on his face.

"He said he'll do it, no problem. He has a holiday home in the Algarve and is used to driving down for the weekend and he'll only charge 120 euros."

I couldn't believe our luck in having found this little gem, considering it was pure chance that he'd been the next cab off the rank when we arrived at the train station a week ago. I suddenly realised how tense I had been and how much the journey home had been worrying me. He had a comfortable Mercedes and was used to driving around Lisbon, and travelling down to the Algarve, the perfect solution.

The rest of the week passed slowly, every day followed a similar pattern, of meals, medication, and physio. Dona Ana and I managed a few conversations in the evenings, once all her visitors had gone and when I felt the loneliest, not having any visitors myself now. On my first evening alone, one of her sons noticed me struggling to eat from my prone position and offered to help. This time I didn't hesitate to accept. Still chatting away to his mum, he washed his hands at the basin in the corner and came to expertly fillet my fish, piling the flesh on one side of the plate with the Dettol vegetables and scraping the bones to the opposite side, out of my limited reach. It was such a kind and unselfconscious gesture, as if totally normal to be cutting up a stranger's food for them. The next night, he didn't even ask, just went and washed his hands and prepared my meal. He

Karen Telling

continued to do so every night for the rest of my stay. I will always remember how grateful I was, when feeling so vulnerable and alone, for that simple action; it cost him nothing but meant everything to me.

18

2004 – A Place of Our Own

As soon as the calendar changed to September, everything felt different, fresher, clearer. The weather seemed lighter, not as heavy and humid as the past few weeks. All the businesses that had closed, for at least the hottest part of the summer, returned. In September, the tourists changed too; older couples or families with babies and toddlers flew in. We could now get our lives in order and move on with the house purchase. Our solicitor called to arrange a date for the promissory contract. It couldn't come soon enough for us; we were itching to live in our own house again.

We were busy in the office too. The diary filled up with appointments, requiring all of us to come in; usually two of us in the office and two conducting viewings and taking on new properties. As predicted, an influx of properties came up for sale, now the most lucrative part of the year had gone but we were still happy with our choice of the little round house.

Nigel and Jenny returned from their summer break, finally able to move into their new house. They came to our place to visit Tink, the grumpy kitten we had rescued from their basement, now a grumpy cat and they invited us to a house warming at their villa.

"It will be your turn next," smiled Jenny.

We kept Tink, of course; still extremely anti-social at the

grand old age of 17. We also kept in touch with Nigel and Jenny, who proved far more sociable and we enjoyed many evenings with them on their trips to Carvoeiro.

My sister, Anne-Marie still had her other part-time job working for The Resident, the local paper. One morning, she turned up a bit late for her work with us.

"I've just had a call from Jane, the editor. She found a little dog at the side of the road this morning."

This grabbed all of our attention. Elaine had recently lost their elderly dog to cancer and missed him terribly.

"Oh, poor thing," she said. "Is it really small?"

"I think so," replied Anne-Marie. "But I didn't have long to talk to her. I'll give her a call at lunchtime and find out more."

However, a few minutes later her phone rang, with more information on the dog. After a quick chat with Jane, she gave us an update.

"She found him on the way to work this morning, just sitting by the side of the road on his own. She's taken him to the vet but he's not chipped so she'll keep him for now, but will try to find him a home."

"Can she send us a photo?" asked Elaine. "We could put a poster up in the window."

"I'll ask. Edward, is it ok if I get a photo emailed here?"

"Yes, of course, my dear. Poor little doggy."

When the photo came through, we all immediately felt sorry for the little chap. He looked a bit of a mixture with short legs and a long body, one ear up and one ear down, whiskery fur on his face, but a smooth-coated body and an overshot lower jaw which made his teeth protrude over his upper lip. You couldn't call him the most handsome dog you'd ever seen, but he did qualify for the cute factor. Elaine was almost in tears looking at the photo.

"Oh, he looks like a little sweetheart!"

We made up a poster, seeking a new home for Jack, as we had already named him, and put it in the office window where plenty of people would see it.

The next morning, Elaine came in and immediately asked about Jack. Anne-Marie checked with Jane; yes, she still had him.

"I spoke to Dave about him last night and showed him the photo. We'd like to go and see him if that's ok?"

"Ok?" said Anne-Marie, "it's more than ok, it would be fantastic if you could take him!"

She whipped out her phone to give Jane the good news.

By coincidence, both Elaine and Jane lived in the same village a little further along the coast, so they arranged to go and see him that evening. Elaine was on tenterhooks all afternoon and Edward ended up letting her leave an hour early, to go and see her boy.

We had just finished eating dinner that evening when my laptop pinged. I had an email from Elaine, copied to Anne-Marie and Edward. No words, just a big photo of her and her husband sitting on Jane's sofa, with Jack stretched out across their laps. They had huge smiles on their faces, including Jack.

The next morning, I took the poster down. Jack didn't need a new home anymore.

19

January 2009, Lisbon

Leaving Hospital

Finally, after a further visit from Theo and passing a walking, sitting, standing test in front of a junior doctor, I was to be allowed home. I rang Nick to start making the preparations. I would be discharged on Friday morning, so he booked a seat on the 7.30 am fast train, which would arrive in Lisbon around two hours later. He had a suitcase full of duvets, pillows and cushions, to make the journey more comfortable for me. I rang José the taxi driver and arranged for him to pick us up around 12.30, as I expected we'd have to wait for prescriptions and letters for my GP.

Leaving hospital always seemed to involve a lot of hanging around, just when you're desperate to get out of there. It turned out no different this time around. Nick arrived on time and I started to get dressed in proper clothes, glad to leave the enormous pyjamas behind, but still having to wear loose yoga pants, not to annoy my scar. Mario re-appeared and announced he had to remove half my staples, an unexpected development, however, all completed in about 15 minutes. He left me with alternate staples, which he suggested could be removed in 4-5 days. I'd worry about the logistics of that when it came to it, for the moment the journey home took precedence over all other concerns.

Nick packed all my possessions, then as predicted, we still weren't free to go by 12.30. José seemed very relaxed about the delay; he had booked the whole afternoon for us, so it didn't matter to him when we left.

Around 1.15, the junior doctor appeared with reams of paper, brown envelopes of x-rays, medicines and prescriptions. Another 10 minutes taken up with explanations, then, at last, the all-clear. Back in the mono-footrest wheelchair for the last time, laden down with bags and pieces of paper and with Nick wheeling the suitcase of duvets, we made our way to the exit. The car waited as close to the front door as physically possible and Nick set about arranging the back seat for me. José stood by and watched, slowly shaking his head.

"No, no," he tutted. "That's not enough."

"It's all I could bring on the train," explained Nick, looking exhausted already.

They somehow managed to slide me into the back seat - thank goodness for leather upholstery - and placed a pillow under my head and a duvet over me. José still wasn't happy but he slid into the driver's seat, Nick next to him in the passenger seat, and off we went. It wasn't ideal but we were on our way home. I'd only been away 11 days but it seemed months since I'd seen all my animals and familiar things. I looked forward to home, some privacy and being allowed to do things at my own speed and according to my own timetable.

I realised José was talking to someone on his mobile, hands-free of course and heard a woman's voice reply. I didn't take much notice, assuming it was his wife, or maybe the taxi controller. He finished the call and half-turned in his seat to address me, knowing Nick's Portuguese wasn't quite up to speed.

"That was my wife," he said. "We are going to my house first."

Ok, I thought, a bit strange but maybe he'd forgotten his wallet or something.

"She will bring many pillows and blankets for you."

Eh? She'll do what?

"I told her we need to make you more secure, so we will go to my house and make a better bed for you."

I translated for Nick and we both started to protest but he was having none of it.

"It's no problem, we have plenty and my house is close to the bridge so we won't lose any time."

No point in trying to stop him; he was in control of the car. So, we thanked him and let him do as he wanted. Ten minutes later, we stopped outside a typical whitewashed house and a small woman rushed out, completely covered in bedding. It was impossible to even tell what colour her hair was. The rain started bucketing down so she handed it all over and dashed back inside; we didn't even have time to thank her.

Nick and José opened a back door each and started to stuff both footwells with cushions until they were level with me, then a spiderman duvet was pushed down behind me and another pillow placed under my feet. I was now completely immobile in a duvet cocoon, even if José had to do an emergency stop, I doubt I would have moved an inch. I had to admit it had been a good idea to pick up the extra quilts. I felt so safe and secure that I fell asleep even before we reached the Vasco da Gama bridge and only woke up around 2 hours later when we pulled into a service station. The rain was torrential but my carers braved the downpour to check if I was ok, and re-arranged my cocoon, turning me on my side, and tucking me in.

Another hour later, we arrived home. Fortunately, it was all on the level, with no steps or stairs so I slowly made my way into the house and straight into bed, still fully dressed. Oh, the blessed relief. I'd made it.

Nick went out to pay José and offered him a drink or something to eat, but it was getting dark and he wanted to keep going.

"Just one thing," he said. "Can I go in and see the senhora?"

So, they both appeared in the doorway and José came around to pat my hand, as he had done in the hospital. I was so grateful to him and I hope I expressed it adequately. He really had made the journey so easy and straightforward, when we had imagined a complete nightmare. I heard his car drive away and once again, I drifted off to sleep.

I had no idea of the long road of recovery that lay ahead and how my life would change completely. How I would never again know a pain-free day, never again sit on a chair like a normal person, or be able to walk up or downhill, how I would eventually be described as Totally and Permanently Disabled and spend the majority of my time lying down.

I was just glad to be home. All that lay in the future.

20

September 2003

The Round House

and a New Friend, Barney

With our promissory contract signed and the ten per cent deposit handed over, we knew the little house was ours. We just had to wait for the final contract to be drawn up and an appointment confirmed at the notary, but we could start packing. We went back to the house for another look around and started to make lists of the jobs we would really need to tackle straight away; top of the list, the kitchen; install oven, washing machine and dishwasher and cut some windows.

"Where's your post box, Tom?" asked Nick.

"I haven't got one. I use a PO box at the post office."

"Ok, I think we'd rather have one at the house, I'll look into it."

We had found out it was normal here to have groups of post boxes at the end of each road or development. The postman did his round on a motorbike, delivering the mail for a large number of houses in one go. It also saved him from having to go off down winding lanes in the more remote areas. The householders stopped off on their way home to pick up their post.

Nick went to the Carvoeiro post office to make enquiries. They told him he would have to go up to the Lagoa post office for something as important as a post box. So off he went, full of hope and enthusiasm.

He returned empty-handed there was a national shortage of post boxes and he would have to keep going back and checking.

"Just as well we're not moving in for a couple of weeks," he sighed.

He popped in every few days but always got the same response. A 'sorry' and a shrug of the shoulders. On his next visit, the man greeted him with a big smile.

"We have received a delivery of post boxes."

"Great," said Nick. "Can I have one?"

"Sorry, no, they are all reserved for a new development."

"Why did you tell me you had some?"

"Because it's good news, it means the boxes are arriving again. Soon, Mr Telling, soon."

The day we had been waiting for finally arrived, to sign the deeds and take possession of our little house. We followed our lawyer's car, on the fifteen-minute drive up to Silves, parked up and walked through the cobbled streets to the Notary's office. Tom was already there in the waiting room and we sat and chatted while waiting for our names to be called. Our lawyer went up to the front desk to show that all the paperwork was in order and the taxes had been paid. Each piece of paper was scrutinised, signed, stamped and photocopied.

Finally, they called us into another room, read out the contract, then translated it into English. They asked us if we understood everything and we readily agreed. Our lawyer produced the cheque and handed it to Tom. We signed and initialled pages of documents and then Tom handed us the keys. We had bought our own house, no more renting, the relief felt immense.

Our lawyer left and Tom, Nick and I walked slowly down to the riverfront.

"Let's have a drink to celebrate?" said Tom, so we sat outside a cafe and toasted each other.

We were keen to go straight to the house, even though we weren't moving in until the next day. Tom had a few last items to pick up, so we agreed to meet there in half an hour.

When we pulled up outside, I saw a dog lying by the front door.

"Tom didn't say he had a dog? I didn't notice him before."

"No, neither did I," said Nick. "I wonder who he belongs to."

Tom drew up beside us and the dog ran over to him.

"Hello Barney, where have you been?" he said as he bent down and ruffled his fur.

Something about the dog seemed familiar, but I couldn't place him.

"Is he yours?" I asked.

"No, he sometimes hangs around here but he's a street dog really. There's an elderly Portuguese couple who keep an eye on him and feed him, but he doesn't really belong to anyone. They collect food from the local restaurants and if they see my car, they hang it on the gate; if not, they feed him here," he said, pointing to a battered old plastic washing-up bowl.

Suddenly it struck me.

"Does a young woman ever take him down to the village?"

"Yes, that's my sister, Eva. Sometimes she stays here when I'm in Lisbon."

Barney was the beautiful, well-behaved dog that we had seen from the balcony of our first rental villa. I couldn't believe it, here we were desperate for a dog, and here was Barney waiting at the front door, as if to welcome us home. Needless to say, he was a street dog no longer and we often joke that we don't know whether we bought the house and got Barney free, or vice versa; somehow, I always felt it was his house first. He wasn't a young dog, probably eight or so when we bought the house but he lived with us until he was about 17, and I had been right from the beginning, he was the perfect dog.

Epilogue

Well, we are still in the Algarve. It has had its ups and downs, more bureaucracy, more surgeries, but we're still here.

We have made lots of good friends, but have lived through sad times too. My Dad died in 2016, after a long illness. He is buried nearby, as was his wish; he never wanted to leave Portugal and now he never will. My Mum is still here too with her little band of rescued dogs and cats, and we have continued to rescue, rehome and TNR countless numbers of dogs and cats, including bottle-feeding abandoned pups and kittens.

My condition has not improved at all, and never will now. I spend most of my time lying virtually flat and rarely leave the house on my own. I tried lots of different ways to try to write this book, but most of it was by two-thumbed typing on my phone. I am unable to travel now, but if I have to be 'stuck' anywhere, I'm glad it's here.

I have now taken Portuguese citizenship and Nick will follow soon, such is our love for this beautiful country and its amazing people. We are so glad we took that first holiday all those years ago. Thank you, Rodney and Christine.

The sequel,

Our Little Piece of Paradise

is available now…..

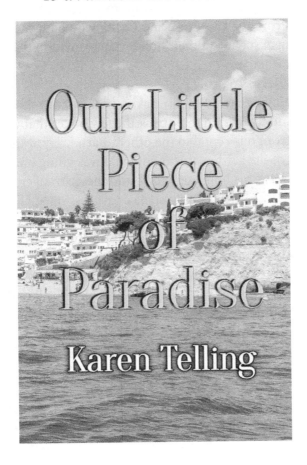

Chapter 1: September 2004, Barney

We often say we don't know if we bought the house and Barney came free, or vice versa. It always felt as if it was his house before it was ours. We moved in a day after signing the deeds, with help from my mum and dad and friends from the U.K., José and Carol, who happened to be in Portugal staying at their holiday apartment in the Eastern Algarve.

It was such a relief to finally have a home of our own again, and we started to unpack the few boxes that we had trailed from one rental to the other. Barney lay at the bottom of the garden, unsure of what was going on. This was his base, his home territory, and these strangers were invading it. He showed no signs of aggression at all, he didn't even bark, but just watched quietly, at a distance. My mum noticed and went to sit beside him. As she stroked his head she reassured him,

"You don't know it yet, but this is probably the best day of your life and the best thing that could happen to you."

He lay his head on his front paws and watched.

It didn't take long to find a place for everything, for now. There was very little storage, just a few kitchen cupboards and a fridge/freezer that we had bought from Tom, the previous owner, but there was no wardrobe or chest of drawers. Anything that couldn't be stored away was stacked in the room that we planned to turn back into a second bathroom. It was just as well we had brought so few belongings with us. Most importantly our antique bedstead was assembled and made up, then Nick went off to pick up a sofa that we had bought from the furniture shop for whom he did deliveries. The next most important people arrived, the satellite TV installers. We had used the same local company several times already. They had installed a system in our rental apartment, and temporary ones in the two houses we had rented, but now we could have our own choice of TV channels. They set to work with ladders and lengths of cables, Barney gave a sigh and turned his back on the noise and the chaos.

Nick arrived back with the new sofa, we had needed a man with a van after all, and some fresh filled rolls and pastries from the local bakery. Seeing the foodmade us suddenly ravenous after all the hard work, so Mum and Carol started handing out lunch and drinks to everyone, using whatever random plates and cutlery, mugs and glasses, that they could find. We all found somewhere to perch around the garden and stopped for a break. Now, this was more interesting for Barney, his nose twitched at the scent of the ham and cheese, and he moved a little closer. Nick broke off a piece of cheese and held it out.

"Come on Barney, do you like cheese?"

Barney hesitated, looking around at all the expectant faces, then gently took the food from Nick's hand. A piece of ham followed, then more cheese, Barney's tail wagged, and we felt him start to trust us.

The house was now as ready as it could be under the circumstances, so Nick and I headed back to the little rental place at Algar Seco to round up the cats, andmake sure we hadn't left anything behind. They all came when we called, and gradually, with a few stragglers, we got them into their travel boxes. As usual, Tink was the last to be caught but some well-placed tuna saved the day. We took a last look around.

"Bye-bye little house, thank you for not letting us down with dodgy plumbing or electrics."

A final look at the beautiful sea view and we locked up and left the keys in the post box as instructed. The cats were complaining loudly as we set off for the five-minute drive home. Home, we were going home.

We knew this would be a test as we didn't know how Barney would react to five cats, but as he didn't come into the house, and we planned to wait a week or two before letting the cats out, we had some time before we had to think about it too much.

What we hadn't thought about was the lack of doors inside. The kitchen, bedroom and bathrooms were fine, but the living room had only saloon type doors, which left a gap at the top and bottom and didn't have any type of lock. We had to get used to closing the back door before opening the kitchen door, and constantly herding cats back into the living room - and you know what they say about herding cats. Although we were heading into October it was still very warm and we were in danger of melting, keeping the house closed up all the time.

"I've had an idea," Nick announced, "if I cut some lengths of wood to about two thirds the width of the windows, we can slot them into the runners in the bottom of the frames, and open the windows enough to get a bit of a breeze, but not enough to let the cats out."

He showed me how the wood could stop the windows opening wider than we wanted, and made a note on his to-do list. This would be a temporary solution but we really needed a proper living room door. The opening was an arch, so the only solution was to have a door custom made. We asked around for recommendations and several people mentioned a carpenter who lived up in the hills beyond Silves. He was happy to take on the job and came down to take measurements. We impressed on him how urgently we needed it, and just over a week later he was back, complete with two doors, each glazed with eight small panels. After a little bit of adjustment they were soon in place, and a perfect fit. They looked great and the whole process had gone so smoothly. We weren't used to this.

Now the cats could be contained, we tried bringing Barney in at night. He wasn't used to coming inside and preferred to sleep on the front porch, wandering in and out of the garden as he felt like it. Our main aim was to keep him safe, and also to stop him from waking everyone up by barking out in the street at 3am, but he wasn't keen. He was able to jump the low front wall, so off he went most days, just coming home for dinner.

He was still being fed by an elderly Portuguese couple who let themselves into the garden and emptied a carrier bag full of restaurant scraps into an old battered washing up bowl. This consisted of a mixture of chicken carcasses, rice, chips, and slices of bread and butter. Barney wolfed it all down, cooked bones and all, something we would never give our dogs, but he had obviously thrived on this diet for years. After a few weeks, we managed to make them understand that we would take responsibility for Barney now, and they no longer needed to feed him.

Barney's best friend was a Husky cross called Nikas, who lived a few houses away. She was also an escape artist and regularly jumped walls and dug tunnels to run free with him. Her owner just couldn't find a way to keep her in the garden and eventually gave up, so she was another night-time barker. Now the cats were safely tucked up in the living room overnight, we tried to get them both inside, but it took a lot of persuasion and countless cubes of cheese and slices of ham to get them to even step over the threshold. The back door stood open all day when we were at home, and we took every opportunity to coax them in, but as soon as we tried to shut the door, Barney panicked and scratched madly to get back outside. This was going to take time.

The other issue was Barney's beautiful long coat, which was matted and full of grass seeds. He was quite a chunk and we didn't fancy trying to groom him ourselves, so found a mobile dog groomer advertised in one of the local papers, and arranged an appointment. I explained that he was basically a street dog and not used to being shampooed and brushed, but Sergio was willing to give it a go. He arrived a few days later and set up a table in the garden, laying out his shampoo, brushes and clippers, while I filled a bucket with warm water. Barney was lifted onto the table, all 35kg of him. I don't think anyone had ever lifted him before but whether it was the surprise at being hoisted onto a table, or just his usual stoicism, he stood still and made no attempt to jump down. Sergio started to gently comb out his thick undercoat, and realised that he was absolutely covered in ticks.

"Come and look at this!" he exclaimed, "I've never seen anything like it."

As he parted the fur I could see the swollen bodies of the ticks, with their heads buried deep in Barney's skin, it must have been so painful for him. Sergio brought out a bottle of surgical spirit and poured most of it into a large tumbler. With a specially designed tick removal tool, he started the slow process of easing the ticks out, taking care not to leave the heads inside. They are horrible creatures, parasites that drain their host of blood, and we soon lost count of how many ended up squashed and drowned in the tumbler.

Two hours later, Sergio pronounced Barney a tick-free zone and lifted him down for a quick comfort break. It was tiring work and he hadn't even started to groom him yet. Back up on the table, Barney was as patient as ever as his coat was shampooed, dried, cut and clipped. His calm acceptance of all this fuss and attention after years of street living was just incredible. There was no hint of aggression, not a growl or a whine, he must have sensed that it would be worth it in the end. At last, it was over and Sergio gave him a final spritz of doggy perfume before lifting him back down onto terra firma. Barney ran off, tail wagging, and promptly rolled in the dusty earth below the hibiscus hedge.

To keep up-to-date with life in Carvoeiro...
and for a photo album to accompany this book please
go to **www.facebook.com/karentellingwriter**
or scan the QR code below

If you have enjoyed *Our Little Piece of Paradise*
or *Another Day in Paradise...*
I would be grateful if you could leave a rating or
review on Amazon or Goodreads, thank you.
Scan the QR code below for my Amazon Author page

Acknowledgements

I first started writing this book years ago, at least five, maybe more. Since then I have retired, and then lock down came along, and I picked it back up again. However, I wouldn't have got to the end without my beta readers and cheerleaders, Ellen, Anne-Marie and Rhona. Thank you for all the help and encouragement and the reminders to get writing.

We are grateful to Dr Carlos Costa and his daughter and successor, Dra Filipa Costa for looking after all our waifs and strays in good times and bad.

Also to Alison Hales, my physiotherapist, who initially diagnosed the severity of my situation, introduced us to my neurosurgeon and accompanied us on that first appointment with him.

Thank you to MTP Publishing for all the help and support in getting the book knocked into shape. Karolina for the amazing cover, just as I imagined it, Caroline for making sense of my scribblings, and Keith for coordinating everything.

Finally, we owe a big thank you to all the people who have helped us along this journey, far too many to mention, but I think you all know who you are.

Available worldwide from Amazon

Made in the USA
Columbia, SC
12 January 2024

30349046R00124